Things I Know
or
Think I Know
or
Thought I Knew
or
Who Knows?

ARTHUR L. STERNE, PH.D.

4 - 09

iUniverse, Inc.
New York   Bloomington

Things I Know or Think I Know or Thought I Knew or Who Knows?

iUniverse books may be ordered through booksellers or by contacting:

iUniverse
1663 Liberty Drive
Bloomington, IN 47403
www.iuniverse.com
1-800-Authors (1-800-288-4677)

ISBN: 978-1-4401-2154-8 (pbk)
ISBN: 978-1-4401-2156-2 (cloth)
ISBN: 978-1-4401-2155-5 (ebk)

Printed in the United States of America

iUniverse rev. date: 2/10/2009

In Loving Memory of my Wife, Carol Ann Sterne,
and for
Charley, Elizabeth, and Savannah Sterne

Acknowledgements

Special recognition and thanks go to all the members, past and concurrent with my membership, of the memoirs group at All Souls Unitarian Church in Indianapolis, Indiana, for their support and encouragement. They include Mary Branson, Jean Petranoff, Don Somers, Sylvia and Ron Reichel, Jane Perry, Phil and Marjorie Snodgrass, Shari Robinson, Judie Ney, Charles Yeager, Elinor Clark, Rosalie Gordon, Barbara Blumenthal, and those members no longer with us--Barbara and Courtney Robinson, Connie Roudebush, Phil Blumenthal, and Ann Sterne. I wish these last five were still alive so that I could thank them for laughing in all the right places (or crying, as the case may be.)

A special thanks to Doris Cantrell, who in addition to being a member of that group, became a very special friend. She went over many of the memoirs in detail and used her considerable skills as a former high school teacher to correct misspellings, grammar, and a misspent word or two. She sometimes added a few editorial comments, which made them more readable and, I hope, enjoyable.

Contents

Introduction

About eight years ago, my late wife Ann and I were invited to join a memoirs group at All Souls Unitarian Church, which we used to attend. We already knew some of the people in the group, and they became very supportive and encouraging of our writing. I quit the group when my wife's illness became severe but then started going back after she died. Ann died in February, 2004, and that date forever divides my life - everything either happened before that or after that. One memoir was given the title, *My Last Memoir,* because at the time I wrote it, I thought it was the last. Time proved me wrong, however, and I went on to write quite a few more. While all the memoirs were written in the last eight years, they contain passages about me when I was as young as five years old and as old as I am now.

Just when you think you've gotten things figured out, not completely, of course, but enough so that you feel confident about yourself and your abilities, or lack thereof, and feel that you don't have to prove anything to anyone anymore, life throws you a curve. We had known that Ann, to whom I'd been married forty-four years, would probably die before I did, but one can never tell for sure about these things. She had leukemia and then non-Hodgkin's lymphoma for eleven years, but she just kept bouncing back after each round of radiation or chemotherapy right up until the end. Ann was always my most loyal cheerleader, and if it weren't for her, I'd have never completed this book.

I've always been curious about things and people - I guess that's why I became a psychologist. I've always asked a lot of questions, not that I thought I was going to find all the answers, but the journey just seemed more interesting that way. Most of my memoirs have questions in them, either implicit or explicit. Most are still unanswered but maybe I've found answers to a few, so why not pass this information along?

All the incidents and anecdotes in this book are true, as best as I can remember them, but I'm seventy-three now, so there may be some details that are slightly off. I've tried to be meticulously honest and accurate, so that I've written about some things that might make someone feel uncomfortable.

I've changed a few names and locations, not just to protect the guilty (or the innocent) but to avoid any unnecessary embarrassment or hurt for anyone.

A few of the memoirs seem surreal, such as the one about the questionnaire asking if one was allergic to mouse protein, but none were made up. Truth, indeed, is often stranger than fiction.

As Henri Frederick Amiel said, "Life is short and we do not have too much time to gladden the hearts of those who travel with us, so be swift to love and make haste to be kind."

Damnyankee

I was born in Hudson Falls, New York when it was twenty-two below zero. Because of all the snow on the ground, I was born at home. When I was just six weeks old, my mother, who had gone to New York only temporarily, returned to Savannah, Georgia, where we lived a couple of years before moving to Jacksonville, Florida, my home until I went away to college. I don't know how frequently people are born in one place and then move to another in such a short time, but there must be lots - children of people in the military, children of refugees, whatever. However, the fact that I was born in the North and grew up in the South was one of the defining characteristics of my childhood. I never wanted to be classified or stereotyped as a Southerner, and I always asserted even when very young that I was a Yankee. To a lot of my family members, particularly the ones who lived in that very insular antebellum city, Savannah, Yankee was a somewhat derogatory term, not just a regionally descriptive term. People there joked that damnyankee was really just one word, and they always uttered it that way.

As a youngster, I took the train to visit relatives in Savannah every summer. I liked going there, as Savannah was not like any other city I'd ever been to, and in my childhood I visited lots of ports where my father's ship came in - New York, Boston, Baltimore, Tampa, Morehead City, N.C. - so I felt as though I had some knowledge for comparison. Being the first grandchild and the only boy, as it turned out, let me have some privileges the other grandchildren didn't get. My grandmother, aunt, and uncle all lived together in a great big house, where there were fig and pecan trees in the side yard, and a large porch on the front where we sat part of almost every afternoon. When I was there, there was no altering of their usual activities just because they had a child visiting. So Friday nights were spent at their poker club, and Tuesday nights were spent at the big old Gothic train station, to which we traveled by streetcar. My grandmother and aunt dressed in their pink and white Red Cross uniforms and ran a canteen for soldiers who were coming in on troop trains and couldn't leave the train station, because they were on their way overseas. Hundreds of egg salad sandwiches and coffee and lemonade were served until the last train left, usually about 1 AM, when we caught the last streetcar home. For years and years after the war, my grandmother and aunt received letters and cards from the servicemen they'd met for only those brief periods of time distributing sandwiches.

Other summers were spent at Savannah Beach, or Tybee Island as it was called by the locals. It was eighteen miles away, through the marshes and over a causeway lined with palm trees and oleander bushes. My grandmother prepared all the meals for my uncle, who had some sort of mysterious illness connected to the first world war, and required a different menu. My aunt got up early each morning and rode the bus into town, where she operated a beauty parlor on one of the downtown squares. Because she was not at home for the midday meal, the main meal was at night, differing from their routine in the city, where my aunt took the bus or streetcar home for midday dinner form 2:00 to 3:00 PM every day.

After lunch at the beach, I couldn't go right into the water; those days, one had to wait at least an hour. My grandmother and I would sit on the seawall and watch the tide come in or go out - just sit there staring at the ocean and occasionally talking about life in general, regardless of the difference in our ages. She'd often grab my knee and squeeze it, saying in her southern drawl, "Ain't this the life?" And I always replied, "It sure is."

Picnics

Life's no picnic, but sometimes it can be. Some of my best childhood memories involve going on picnics. Picnics were fun, and we always looked forward to them. Just the word "picnic" has pleasant, fun connotations. The word makes you think of sunny images, food in abundance, the outdoors, trees, and water - a lake, river, or even the ocean.

The best picnics I can remember from early childhood involved a place called Rockaway Beach, near the very tip of northern Florida. It was on the St. John's River and although most of Florida is flat, there were small cliffs or embankments there. Long, twisted vines hung from ancient trees and sometimes if they were placed right, you could use them to propel yourself out over the water and then drop in.

There might be lemonade in a big, porcelain jug with a spout, or maybe there were lots of cold bottled soft drinks in a tub of ice - ice that had been bought in a large block and then chipped away with an ice pick and packed solidly around the drinks. It was really a joy to reach way into the bottom of the tub and find the coldest bottle of the kind of drink you wanted - an RC cola, a Nehi orange, a Grapette, or a root beer. There would be watermelon sometimes and at other times, homemade ice-cream in an old-fashioned churn that everyone took turns cranking. Sometimes there was fried chicken, potato salad, and red rice, but when the picnic was planned on short notice, there were sandwiches that tasted wonderful, even if they were on just plain old white bread. Maybe there were wieners that would be heated on sticks over a fire or small grill and made into hot dogs. In the South in those days, it wasn't a *hot dog* until there was a bun around it. Mustard and cole slaw were the only things put on them - no catsup, sauerkraut, or chili, as done up North. Lemon pie, chocolate cake, or maybe cupcakes or brownies were often brought along, with fresh peaches or strawberries to put into the ice cream.

My love of picnics has survived and changed somewhat over the years. I remember my first picnic in Indiana - on an autumn day in a state park. It seemed a little strange to me because the main food was chili, which had to be heated on a small grill.

Usually, picnics involved family members. For several years, we had picnics at Eagle Creek Park where Ann and I would go early on the morning of July 4th to find a spot that overlooked the water. We'd spread out lawn chairs and a couple of quilts to reserve the space for the others, who would show up at varying times of the morning or early afternoon.

There'd be canoeing or just plain old rowing in rented boats, and of course, the traditional horseshoes that I always brought along and usually insisted everyone play, even those who said they'd never played or didn't remember how. We'd play in teams, with adults and children on each team.

People seem either to like picnics or they don't. The ones who don't, complain of the ants or the flies or the sand. Once I heard a woman say that she wished the entire world was paved with asphalt so that she wouldn't have to go on a picnic ever again. I think what she was really saying, though, was that she didn't like big family gatherings - there was too much of a chance for family squabbling or old conflicts to arise. People seem to let their hair down on a picnic, both literally and figuratively, and are perhaps more relaxed and candid in the open atmosphere of the woods or the wilds. Insects and poison ivy aren't the only obstacles to a successful family picnic, and I'm willing to chance that to go on another picnic.

Garland and Dietrich

Judy Garland always made a big entrance down the center aisle when she performed, but she couldn't do that at Clowes Hall, the concert hall on the Butler University campus, because it doesn't have a center aisle. Nevertheless, she made a splashy entrance anyway, with a big voice, perhaps enhanced by a microphone, but it seemed genuine at the time. Garland and Dietrich were people with real charisma, and they could captivate an audience from the moment they got on the stage until they left, and then some. We saw both of them at Clowes Hall in the mid-1960's.

The night that we saw Marlene Dietrich, a small ensemble group, not bad but not noteworthy either, played classical music for about forty-five minutes before the curtain came down for a brief intermission. The crowd grew somewhat antsy, since an hour had passed and there was no sign of the headliner. Then, she came out in a slinky gown that gave the illusion of being transparent, trailing about a twelve-foot fox fur and sang quite a diverse group of songs - her standards from her early movies, such as *Lola* and *Lili Marlene,* but also new ones, such as *Go ' Way From My Window, Where Have All the Flowers Gone?,* and *Puff, the Magic Dragon.* She stood up clutching the microphone on a stand in front of her and sang for exactly one hour; interspersed was a lot of banter with the audience, asking which song we wanted her to sing next, and telling about how she happened to choose this or that particular song to sing. At the end of the sixty minutes, there was thunderous applause, and a standing ovation, while she took bow after bow, and thanked the audience, but it soon became apparent that she was not going to include an encore. After a great deal more applause, she finally wrapped herself up in the large stage curtain and slowly left the stage, only to return once more and start receiving dozens and dozens of red roses, brought to her by handsome young ushers, who literally loaded the stage with them. She held one bouquet, and the others were placed at her feet, taking up almost the entire stage in front of the curtain.

Shortly after this, in 1964, we heard Judy Garland on the Jack Paar Show, and she was in the middle of describing Dietrich's big ego, as she put it. She said she had seen Dietrich in London recently, and showing a bit of rivalry, told of how Dietrich had brought a recording to a party they were both attending and had played it for the other guests. Thinking it was going to be some of her songs recorded for different audiences, the guests were paying rapt attention, but it turned out to be a record of only the applause at each place Dietrich had played, "Here is the applause in Paris," " Here is the applause in Berlin," " Here is the applause in Frankfort." Most listened politely and some could see the differences, because how people applaud in most European countries is quite different from that in the U.S. - everyone there claps in unison, for example.

Later, I read in a biography of Dietrich by her daughter that every seemingly spontaneous remark, gesture, utterance, etc. was memorized and delivered exactly the same way in each of Dietrich's performances. Men were placed in the audience to call out names of songs, for example. I bought a record of Dietrich's, and it was true—every single word was exactly the same as when we had seen her performance here, every question the same. She had several of the most successful concert tours of any single performer, particularly one at her age, and after her movie career had almost ended. Her daughter also said that college students were usually hired and dressed as ushers and that all the roses brought to the stage had been ordered by Dietrich herself and were part of the act in each city. In fact, she was somewhat of a skinflint, and if the roses could be used the next night, too, she had them taken to the next town in which she was performing. I much preferred the illusions, and that's what I try to remember as I listen to the recordings now.

Growing Up and Away

I couldn't wait to grow up - to grow up and all that I thought that meant - to leave, to get away, to see and do new things, to be independent. My whole childhood seemed like a waiting period. I never thought, during my childhood, that I'd ever look back and wish for childhood again or think that those years would ever be described as being happiest or even happier than later years. I never think this now, either. It wasn't that my childhood consisted of lots of horrible events or traumatic experiences; in fact, it was a fairly ordinary childhood compared with most others. It was just that my expectations of the future were so much more attractive and appealing.

When I went to college, only 75 miles away - to the University of Florida campus in Gainesville - it seemed a world away. I never got homesick and rarely went home after then except on holidays or during the summer months. I wouldn't have gone then if I had had somewhere else to go, and I frequently did. I never skipped a class to leave early for any of the breaks, and after the first year would return to campus on Friday after Thanksgiving, where I would find the campus and library and Student Union open because there were so many foreign students or students from out of state who didn't go home at all. I always used the excuse of having to work on term papers or other projects that required me to be on campus, and this was not entirely untrue. I spent most of that extra time doing just those things or doing more studying. Of course, a lot of classmates went home to see all their friends who had gone to other colleges far away, such as Duke or Emory, but usually only at Christmas, because they had their breaks at different times from the colleges in Florida.

The University of Florida campus was beautiful in the Spring, which often started early. There were rows and rows of azaleas, of every imaginable color, but especially pink, lavender, and purple, dogwoods, redbuds, oleander bushes, magnolias, and all sorts of oak trees with Spanish moss hanging down. Most of the older buildings had ivy growing on them. Summer, of course, came early, too, and there were trips to the beach or to the lake just a few miles south of the campus that the university owned and operated for the use of students and faculty.

I walked a lot during those years, as it was a big campus, one of the largest land grant college campuses in the nation. I often walked downtown, as the downtown contained the only two movie theaters in town, and the bus service was slow and erratic.

I still do a lot of walking. I've lived in Indiana since 1961. Every time I drive out of the state, on the way home, as I approach the Indiana state line, I feel as though I've come back home. It's a long way from my childhood home, but I guess I've truly grown up and away at last.

Windows

Windows are interesting, both architecturally and psychologically. Windows frame, but also focus, your view of the world, give it structure or stability, like a camera might do, except the scenes through windows are in constant change. Windows also limit what you are able to see as well. How many times have you read a book or short story that mentioned someone sitting beside some sort of window or seen a movie with someone appearing at a window, or peering out or in?

My bedroom in the house in Florida where I spent most of my childhood had eight windows. There were two walls with four windows each; they weren't large windows, but each set of two opened in and attached to each other with a latch like you used to see on wooden screen doors. I used to lie in bed and watch the skies - lots of stars on some nights and lots of thunder and lightning on other nights. They allowed the cool air in on hot nights, but they also let the cold air in on cold nights - cold for northern Florida, anyway.

My bedroom faced the backyard, and in the summer I could see our small vegetable garden. Right outside, so that sometimes its limbs thrashed the screen, was a huge old camphor tree, the kind that you could crush its leaves and get the smell of camphor, a smell one could never forget over all these years now. It was a huge tree with lots of limbs that cats often climbed, particularly when they were fighting. Sometimes the only way to get the cats to stop their fighting was to turn the hose on them. The other big tree to the side of the house that I could see was a crepe myrtle. In the spring it had large clumps of pink, almost fuchsia-colored, flowers and also Spanish moss. Another tree that I could see from the windows that faced the back was a holly tree that was actually in the yard next door but it hung way over into our yard. It was green all year but never had any red berries. We were told that it was because it was a male tree or that there needed to be two trees together to have berries on them.

Our detached garage and the fence were covered with a vine with little pink flowers. It started out in the spring with just a few leaves on tendrils and by August, it had covered half the garage and the entire fence, so that you couldn't even see the posts or the wire. Soon it started to die and within a very short time, less than two weeks, it had gone entirely. My view on the other side was more colorful, as several years before an elderly couple who had just married moved in and was going to start a nursery, so they planted the entire sides and back yard in azaleas - in almost every color imaginable. Then they found out about zoning laws and that they couldn't sell them as they had planned.

From the windows in our front yard, you could see more crepe myrtles, and just past the sidewalk were two palm trees; but these were very much overshadowed by the huge live oak tree that again hung over from next door and had long grey clumps of Spanish moss and provided so much shade that the palm on that side of the yard only got about half as big as the other palm that got more sun. Of course, we got lots of acorns and leaves, but the oak tree never lost all its leaves even in the coldest part of the year.

I can't imagine working in a place without windows. I was fortunate to have worked in a hospital for many years that was designed so that each patient's room and each office faced the outside and had at least one large window. Of course, corner offices were coveted because they usually had more windows. I'll bet anyone who lived or worked at the same place for several years could conjure up a memory of the views from familiar windows. It's not something one forgets.

Those Were the Days or Were They?

I remember when I lived on Dellwood Avenue in the 1940s and '50s that we almost never locked our front doors or even closed them unless it was really cold. Even when we did lock the doors, many of the windows were often left open because of the heat, especially upstairs in a home in northern Florida that was not air-conditioned. Those times seem long gone now when we lock our doors and then deadbolt them to make sure no one breaks in. We lived in a big two-story house on an older tree-lined street with sidewalks. Many of the neighbors had lived there for years. There were a few apartments, usually just two to a building, and even the people who rented had been there a long time. I'm sure if anyone did try to break into our house, one of our neighbors would have seen what was happening and done something about it.

We walked to a lot of places in those days - a small shopping center with a movie theater, drugstore, bakery, dime store, hardware store, even a shoe store, and several apparel stores. There were three large parks near enough for us to walk to, and each had its own distinct character. The farthest one called Willow Branch Park was the largest and had a branch of the library there. I always liked its name. In May, the Episcopal Church that I and my family attended, The Church of the Good Shepherd, always put on a May Fair, with each group of children in a certain grade playing a different type of animal or mythical creature, so that costumes had to be made and worn. In one section of the park, hedges were grown in a semi-circle to give the effect of an outside stage. It was in a section of town called Avondale.

One of the other parks, called Memorial Park, was on the St. Johns River and had a fountain and marble statues in the fountain and around the sides. It was a very formal park, suitable for taking pictures of dressed up individuals and families on special occasions, such as weddings or at Easter. It was in a section of town called Ortega. Many of the street names in this entire part of the city were named after Native American tribes that had been in the area (and some who weren't) such as Seminole Avenue and Apache Street. It didn't have any playground equipment, but you could watch the ships and sailboats on the river and see a draw bridge open to let some of the larger yachts through. There were paths through the immaculately tended grounds around a big open space that went the entire length of the park.

The other park, Riverside Park, had the same name as the section of town where we lived. It was adjacent to the shopping center, called Five Points, because one of the intersections had five streets crisscrossing it. There were busy streets all around it, with lots of traffic, including buses and taxis. It had a lot of playground equipment and a big pond with ducks. When we were small, we went to play at one of the parks almost weekly.

In the summers, we often had a small vegetable garden, with beets, carrots, lettuce (which never did well) green beans, radishes, and tomatoes. I remember all the weeding and watering that it took to make the vegetables prosper. Bushes and trees, even palm trees, had to be pruned during the summer months, so I was always busy working in the yard. Of course, driving by that house recently, the yard looked very small, although the house still looked large.

We had a big front porch with a swing and several rocking chairs, and we often sat outside during the early evenings. Neighbors went for walks and would often stop and chat with us. People didn't run or jog or even walk at a fast pace, just sort of lumbered along, admiring the flowering trees, the edged lawns, and the flowers in bloom. Even though many of the dogs in the neighborhood were in fenced-in yards or taken for walks only on leashes, there were still many dogs and cats that roamed the neighborhood. Occasionally, there would be a cat or dog fight. Sometimes one of the adults would have to get a garden hose and turn it on a couple of cats who would be fighting way up in a tree. These were usually males fighting over a female. A cat occasionally would get on the roof, and no amount of coaxing would get it off. I can tell you from experience that all cats do not land on their feet when they fall, although the part about having nine lives might be true.

We went to a little corner grocery (where all the items were priced much higher than at the supermarkets) to buy last minute items - fresh bread, ice-cream, or fresh fruit, or something my mother or grandmother had run out of - salt, baking soda, Crisco - things used to make cakes and pies and brownies. Desserts were almost always served with the main meal of the day, which was supper on weekdays and dinner on Sundays.

We didn't have CNN but we did have two newspapers a day; the afternoon paper had more local news and happenings. The newspapers were always full of war stories - not much different from today, really. It seems we had more time each day - days weren't as full as they are today, although we did a lot of the same things. We always had meals together and sat around the table and talked during the meals, especially the evening meal. Sometimes the topics became quite heated and arguments occurred.

People didn't seem to go in as many different directions, although various members of the family went to various groups and had different activities. I remember being in Cub Scouts, then in the Boy Scouts, taking swimming lessons at our church, which had a huge indoor swimming pool, then later being in DeMolay, where I was the chaplain, believe it or not. My sisters were in Campfire Girls and later belonged to a high school sorority, which was strictly forbidden, even though everyone knew about them and who was in them and where they met. For some reason, they were not legal, though. The girls would have car washes on Saturdays to raise money for their activities, so they weren't exactly secret societies. Of course, they were all white because the schools were still segregated, as were the various communities. Once in a while, a family of a different race lived in one of the segregated communities, and it was usually because one of the members of the family was white. Nevertheless, the children still had to go across town to the all-black school.

Maybe these were the good old days only part of the time.

The Best Laid Plans

I thought I had things all figured out. I'd stay at the University of Florida where I'd gotten my B.A. degree and get a Ph.D., but just to be on the safe side I'd go ahead and do the master's thesis and get a Master's Degree, too, in case something happened that I didn't finish my doctoral degree. I knew almost all the professors and most of the graduate students, and I felt comfortable and knew what was expected. I thought I had a very good chance of getting financial help, either a full scholarship or a fellowship, where you had to work fifteen hours a week. I could be an assistant to one of several professors I liked and get experience teaching or doing research under their guidance. Thus, I was really thrown off balance and couldn't believe the rumor I heard circulating that was finally put into writing in a memo and posted on the Psychology Department bulletin board. No one, it said, could obtain three degrees in the same subject at the university any more. And here I was, ready to finish my Master's Degree, after just a year and a half, so that I would get my M.S. in January and then just slide into the Ph.D. program.

I went to my advisor and several other psychologists on the faculty and discussed the matter, and they all said it was some new dean's idea and that we would all just have to go along with it. In fact, they all encouraged me to apply to some other prestigious universities that they knew about or where former students had gone. I poured over information and finally applied to Duke, University of Maryland, University of North Carolina, and Vanderbilt University. Since I wanted to start in mid-year, I was worried that I wouldn't be able to get any financial help, but I was offered money and other enticements at all of them. I finally chose Vanderbilt, partly because of its reputation and partly because they offered me money that didn't have any strings attached and no work or teaching requirements for the first year.

I tried to find another student with a car who was going to Nashville, Tennessee, over the semester break and was lucky enough to do so. We had to leave early one Tuesday morning and planned to take turns driving straight through. I'd never been to Tennessee, so the hills were new to me. We finally got to Nashville about midnight; we were hungry and needed coffee, so we stopped in an all night hamburger place. We asked the waitress if she knew where Vanderbilt was and if we were anywhere near it, as I had an appointment the next day to see about housing. She said she'd heard about Vanderbilt, in this slow southern drawl, much more Southern and slow than the people sounded in Florida, I noticed, but she didn't know exactly where it was.

There was a very heavy fog, and you could barely see across the street from one side to the other. We didn't feel like looking around a great deal, and the guy who was going to see his girlfriend at another college in Nashville was anxious to get going. I had seen a sign on an old three-story brick house that said, "Rooms for Rent," so I went back and got a room there for the night, lugging all my suitcases, boxes of books, and a huge trunk up two flights of stairs. Surprised was my reaction, when I woke up the next morning, pulled back the blinds and looked directly across the street into a college campus, that just from the looks of it, had to be the Vanderbilt campus.

Some of the first correspondence I had with former classmates at the University of Florida informed me that I could have gotten an exception to the rule, since they were not applying it to current students who would have been able to get all three degrees if they were currently enrolled.

Maybe it was fate, however, that intervened, because unbeknownst to me, six months earlier, Ann had decided that besides an R.N., she wanted a Bachelor's Degree. So she applied to three universities--Duke, University of North Carolina, and Vanderbilt. She had already obtained a National League of Nursing scholarship that could be used almost anywhere she wanted to go; I don't need to tell you which one she chose and where she would be starting her second semester in a few days.

The South I Remember

Sitting on the front porch of my grandmother's house in Savannah, Georgia, on late summer mornings, I would hear women's voices calling out in a sing-song fashion, "Fresh butter beans, black-eye peas, turnip greens." It seems I also heard … "watermelon," but I wonder about that because the people doing the calling-out were black women with baskets on their heads, and surely watermelons would have been too heavy. I seem to remember that an open truck with shelves of fruits and vegetables packed in ice would be following them, so maybe the watermelons were on it.

My grandmother would tell me to call her when I heard them coming, so I'd run to find her - in the kitchen or out in the backyard in a small building where she would be washing clothes, where there was always the strong odor of bleach. She might be hanging out the wash on the clothesline with old-fashioned wooden clothes pins or adjusting the lines with big poles to push them higher in the air to catch the breeze, I guess.

She would then prepare a huge dinner for me and her and my aunt Zaida, who rode the streetcar home from her beauty shop downtown each day at 2 PM. My aunt would spend an hour at home and then return to her shop to work several more hours. My uncle would be there, too, and he always needed specially prepared foods, such as slimy boiled okra instead of the fried okra the rest of us had. He was thin, had ulcers, and a sunken-in chest. He wheezed and coughed a lot, and I was told he had been mustard-gassed in the First World War and had only one lung. Nevertheless, he continued to smoke.

Uncle Edwin collected stamps and sometimes showed me his many books of them - some new, but most cancelled, although meticulously kept and fastened magically, it seemed, to the pages in books made specifically for that purpose. A few years later when he died, I was given his stamp collection, and my mother put it away. I later learned she had destroyed the entire collection because she had been afraid that he had suffered from tuberculosis and that I could catch TB just by handling the books and stamps.

In contrast to my uncle, who wasn't very social, my grandmother and great aunt and I would go out almost every day that I was there on a summer visit. I don't think they changed their schedule for me, but we'd all go downtown in the evening to Morrison's Cafeteria. Some afternoons we'd go to a Red Cross luncheon at the Pink House on Oglethorpe Square, one of the many squares in downtown Savannah. My grandmother would take me to movies or to Daffin Park to go swimming, or to the hospital to help roll bandages for the war effort. We went to friends' houses to play baccarat or to my other aunt and uncle's place on the river, called Swimchat, out near Isle of Hope. Built during the late 1930's, Swimchat consisted of a small house right on the river, and it had a floating dock that was even with the house and deck during high tide but which you had to go down an almost vertical ladder to get to when the tide was low. Your car had to be parked in the surrounding woods and then you had to go out over a long, built-up walkway that went through the marshes and was covered with oyster shells.

The South, the South I remember, was full of porches, especially screened porches, Spanish moss hanging down from huge oak trees, marshes, dark rivers, breezes, a certain loneliness and idealism and sadness. On the darker side, it was about prejudice, small minds, intolerance, insularity, pretending, and superstition. It was also about individuality, eccentricity, story-telling, white lies that no one really believed, manners, and superficial politeness. But it wasn't about something that was easily forgotten, that's for sure.

Tuesdays Off

Six days a week from 11 AM to midnight, or even later on weekends, at a starting salary of $32 a week, with Tuesdays off - who in his right mind would work those hours for those wages? I did, for three summers in the 1950s. I mainly waited on tables, but I also helped cook and washed dishes when they needed me to do those things. Of course, I did get a couple of hours off between 2 and 4 PM, free meals and lodging, free laundry, and even the use of my uncle's brand new Kaiser one summer. If you remember the Kaisers and Frazers made in the fifties, you know why my uncle had it only a couple of years. It was a big wide piece of junk that could seat four in the front seat. But using it on some of those hot summer afternoons was great.

I also made more money in tips than I made in salary, and in my last summer there I got a raise to $39 a week and half of my aunt's profits from the juke box.

Early in June I would take the train from Florida to New Jersey, using a ticket my Aunt Dot and Uncle Henry had sent me, but I would have to pay my own way home. They owned a seafood restaurant about half-way between New York City and the Jersey shore. So the weekends were busy with people on their way to the shore or to the horse races at Asbury Park. Many of these same people returned to the restaurant on their way home Sunday night. The restaurant was in a little town called Morgan, about 90 per cent of whose inhabitants were Roman Catholic. In those days Catholics all ate fish on Fridays, so the townspeople bought cooked fish by the pound, as well as quarts of cole slaw and Manhattan clam chowder, making Friday the busiest day of the week at the restaurant.

My aunt was from Savannah, Georgia, and had been a Baptist. My uncle was from Canada, and he was a Roman Catholic. They met at a resort in upstate New York where each had gone to seek better employment. Two more different people, you wouldn't find. My uncle was a dreamer. My aunt was the practical one, attending to all the nitty-gritty details of running a restaurant, making sure we didn't run out of napkins or cocktail sauce. She also devised cost-cutting devices, such as watering down the catsup or wanting to salvage a huge pot of clam chowder that she had scorched slightly. My uncle would never let her do this, though. Wearing his long white apron and chef's hat, my uncle schmoozed the customers with a special plate of a few Cherry Stone clams on the half-shell or some fresh lobster tail dipped in warm butter. They literally and figuratively *ate it up* and were repeat customers.

It happened that Tuesday was often the slowest day of the week, so that's why I got Tuesdays off. I would get up much earlier than usual on Tuesdays and take the bus into the next little town, which was Perth Amboy, and board a train to New York City. One day I was in a hurry and caught the wrong train, which had stopped only for a minute to load passengers and then sped on. I asked someone if the train was going to New York City, and he told me it was not - it was going to Jersey City, but that I should follow him and all the other passengers who were going there, too. So when the train stopped, it appeared to be the end of the line and everyone got off and took a seat in what looked like a waiting area on the dock. Was I surprised when I noticed we were moving. It was a ferry across to the city. I followed the crowd to a subway and got off when I heard someone yell, "Next stop, Times Square." It was better than arriving at Penn Station, which required a taxi to get to Times Square, where I usually started my exploration.

I usually went by myself because everyone else had to work; in fact, they were short one worker because of my being off, so it was no use to ask someone to go with me. It really didn't feel as if I were alone, though, because everywhere I went was crowded with people - people who seemed to be hurrying, determined - people with a purpose.

I was awed by all the things to do and see, particularly when I didn't want to spend much of my hard-earned money, which I was saving for college expenses. The museums and libraries were free. You could take the ferry to the Statue of Liberty for about fifteen cents, ride the subway for a nickel, eat at the Automat for next to nothing. The Observation Deck at the Empire State Building cost only fifty cents. You didn't have to be afraid to go to Central Park in those days, where you could rent a rowboat for two dollars. I always went to a movie, as well, and got a haircut in a different barber shop every other week.

I walked a lot, almost everywhere I went, since I discovered that one cab driver had charged me three times the amount another driver charged to get to the same place - the U.N. Building, which always had interesting exhibits from other countries. I was warned not to look up because people would know I was a gawking tourist, but I couldn't help myself. I was fascinated by two aspects of the city - the people, who looked and dressed differently from anywhere I'd ever been and the architecture - from Gothic cathedrals to ultra-modern skyscrapers. I was shocked, too, to find that Macy's sold whole, uncooked chicken and bakery items on the first floor, right next to bargain items and souvenirs. I found that a lot of the stores were selling overpriced items to tourists.

I usually caught the last bus back, as there were no trains in the evening. It left around 9 PM. and arrived in Morgan a little after 10. I'd stop by the restaurant for a cup of coffee and relate my adventures to the other employees, many of whom I learned had never been to New York City except for a special parade or a baseball game.

I always started Wednesday mornings with a smile on my face, thinking that it would be just six more days until my next adventure into the city - my next Tuesday off.

The Lie

I was about seven years old and old enough to have known better. It started when I happened to look out one of our living room windows and saw one of the most shocking sights I'd ever seen. Coming catty-cornered across the street was Mrs. Kambouris, stark naked. She was holding two washcloths trying to cover parts of her body. This was a rather formal lady who had glistening olive skin and who always wore her hair in a chignon at the back of her head, never a hair out of place. She entered the front door of the home across the side street from us, and a little later we could hear a lot of yelling. I don't remember if I could actually hear what was being said at the time or whether I remember what was told to me afterward. But she yelled at poor old Mr. Kelly to get up out of that bed, because he could walk. Now Mr. Kelly had been bedridden for years, crippled by rheumatoid arthritis, his bony, swollen hands and feet gnarled and painful. Amidst all the yelling, she began to try to pull him out of the bed to his feet.

Next, I heard the siren of an ambulance, and soon two men dressed in white uniforms ran into the house. There was more loud shouting, but this time it was all in Greek, and I couldn't tell what was being said. Just then Mr. Kambouris arrived in his big Buick, parked next to the ambulance, and ran into the house. A little later, the men in white came out carrying a stretcher with Mrs. Kambouris strapped down on it and covered with a sheet. She was yelling at the top of her lungs, in English now, that if her husband didn't make them stop, she was going to call him"…*that name*"—over and over in a loud guttural sound that seemed so different from her usual musical-sounding voice. Then they all got into the ambulance except for Mr. Kambouris, who got into his own car and followed them as they drove away.

I guess it had started earlier when my mother came into the living room where I was playing and said she was going across the street to see if she could borrow a cup of sugar from Mrs. Kambouris. It was wartime and sugar was rationed. She had just dropped and broken a bowl that held the last sugar in the household, and she had wanted to make some cookies. When she got back a little later, there was a lot of hushed talk between her and my grandmother, who lived with us. I then heard some muffled voices on the telephone. Evidently, Mother had gone in the Kambouris's side kitchen door and had found Mrs. Kambouris, with her straight dark hair hanging down over her shoulders, standing at the kitchen sink, singing at the top of her lungs. She had all of her daughter Christina's dolls in the kitchen sink, washing them. All at once she stopped singing, walked over to the screen door, and snapped the lock on it shut. My mother, who usually was prone to become hysterical in crisis situations, calmly began asking her about the dolls and what she was singing and diverted her attention until she got to the kitchen door and unsnapped the lock, saying she had left something in the oven and had forgotten to turn it off, so she had to hurry, but that she would be right back. As soon as she got the door opened, she ran out and back across the street to our house.

She telephoned Mr. Kambouris, who owned a business downtown. He later told my mother that he should have known something was wrong. He suspected something was not right at breakfast when his wife had talked very loudly and had started singing so early in the morning, but then he thought that maybe he was overreacting and that she was just happy because it was such a nice day. After all, he had to get to his business and open it for his customers. Still, he had felt uneasy and had suggested that Christina go play with her cousins, Sophia and Helen, who lived just around the corner.

Several months later I remember my grandmother's talking to Mrs. Mills, the woman who had moved in across the street to care for Christina while her mother was away. Christina was a year younger than I, but older than my twin sisters, who were only three at the time. She was very dark and wore her hair in pigtails down her back. She seemed strange, washing her hair in rain water from a barrel, and she ate unusual food, seemed shy, and didn't engage in any rambunctious play like the rest of us in the neighborhood. She also had to practice the piano every day for at least an hour.

Christina would sometimes come over and show us the gifts her mother had been sending her from some place up north, in Baltimore. I remembered, because just earlier that year I had been on a trip there, where my father's ship had come in for a few days before sailing back on the ocean somewhere. Christina said that her mother was away at a place that was helping her to get better - that she had been very sick and had almost died. Most of the gifts that Christina had received were jewelry, silver bracelets that were shiny and rather misshapen and had strange marks on them. But then they got better and better and looked more like the jewelry one saw in department stores downtown.

One day I was on the other side of the street, trying to talk Christina into getting into my little red wagon with the wooden slatted sides, so that I could take her for a bumpy ride, but she was refusing, saying I would go too fast. She then complained about Mrs. Mills, a woman my grandmother's age, and said she didn't see why she had to have an old lady stay with her who was ugly and didn't know how to cook the food she liked, and she didn't know why her mother had to go away and why she didn't come back home. Before she could finish, I looked at her and said, "Your mother's crazy, and that's why she had to go away, and she's locked up in an insane asylum." She looked at me in disbelief, with sad dark eyes and started crying, then sobbing, saying what I had said was not true, not true at all, and then ran inside. Then my mother called, and I remember telling the first lie that I can truly remember telling. I told her I most certainly did not tell Christina that her mother was crazy. It was a cruel thing to do, and I knew that I had done something wrong, and I learned, much later, not to bring unnecessary hurt into the world.

Been Up to See Moses, Huh?

"Been up to see Moses, huh?" If he had said Judge Moses, we might have understood what he meant, but just saying that... "been up to see Moses, huh?" and then giving a sly, knowing kind of grin, we thought he had been drinking on the job and ignored him for the rest of the short elevator ride. We didn't think anything about the elevator operator's comments, until several days later when we got the marriage certificate that said the ceremony had been performed by Judge Herbert H. Moses.

For weeks, I had been dreading the planned wedding. I hated things that were in any way traditional - at least any ceremonies or formal gatherings. Ann and I had planned a small wedding for the semester break that came about the end of the third week in January. We had not planned to have any family members come up for the wedding, as there were only a few days between semesters, and we would be moving into an apartment, and Ann would be starting a new job, teaching at St. Thomas Hospital in Nashville, Tennessee. We had decided to have a few of our friends, mostly graduate students whom one of us had met during the past year, or year and a half, in Ann's case. The number of people who wanted to come kept growing and growing, and a few even said they planned to stay at Vanderbilt during the break just so that they could attend our wedding.

The minister of the small on-campus Episcopal chapel sent us a letter, saying he was sorry but that he was going to be out of town that week, something he had not been aware of when we had set the date. However, he said, he'd arranged for us to be married by the minister of an Episcopal Church near the campus. At first, we thought, so what? Then we got a letter from the second minister informing us that he would like to meet us and had scheduled a *counseling session* for the following Tuesday evening. He said he made it a point of never marrying a couple unless he had first *counseled* them. The more I read over his letter, the more I didn't care for his arrogant attitude. So, when we met for dinner at the Campus Grill just before going for the counseling session, I discussed with Ann our canceling the session, and then said, "Why don't we just go and get married by a justice of the peace downtown? In fact, why not tonight, since it looks like classes are going to be called off tomorrow because of all the snow piling up?" To my surprise, Ann said, "Why not?" as she seemed bothered somewhat, too, by the number of people who wanted to attend our wedding.

Not having a car, we both went back to our rooms, I to the graduate dormitory and she to the old mansion that was the graduate house for women. An hour or so later, I arrived with my small overnight suitcase in a taxi. Ann came out with a large purse and in boots and overcoat, because by this time, the snow was really piling up. No doubt the taxi driver overheard our conversation, even though we had been trying to talk low enough that he couldn't hear us, because when we pulled up to the Court Building in downtown Nashville, he offered to turn off the meter and wait for us, telling us that we'd never get another taxi in this weather, and telling us that he, too, had been married in night circuit court.

We didn't notice the elevator operator at all on the trip up. When we got to the Judge's office, he said that yes, he was free and could marry us if we had already gotten the license, etc., which we had. He asked if we had brought along any friends for witnesses, and we told him we hadn't. He told us it would be okay and called in two night guards, both of whom had pistols with them when they showed up. The judge must have weighed close to 350 pounds, and just before performing the ceremony, he stopped and said that he had to get his suit jacket, which he always kept available for such occasions. He then put on one of the oldest, dustiest jackets I'd ever seen, and he started the proceedings while Ann was still unfastening her boots. Ann had on a two-piece suit, with a three-quarter length coat, and we wondered if they thought she was pregnant and thus the seemingly quick wedding. When he said that the groom could now kiss the bride, he and the two guards both laughed, looked at her middle, and said in unison, "I bet he's done that before." I gave the judge some money and handed bills to each of the guards, and we headed for the elevator as quickly as we could, where we were asked if we had been up to see Moses.

The Ties That Bind

I hate wearing a tie. For over thirty-five years I wore a tie five or six days a week. I hated the way ties felt; they always seemed too tight. If you have to wear a tie almost every day for years and years, think how many you need, the various colors, and then, of course, the different styles and widths. Ties are narrow or wide with the whim of fashion. I learned that you couldn't keep your old wide ties until wide ties came back into style because the designs were so different when the new wave of wide ties came in. I have no doubt that ties were made to choke men. What corresponds on women? I don't know, unless it would be high heels or bras or girdles. At least two of those had a function. Wouter vanWinden, whoever he was, said of ties, "No piece of clothing combines so little function with so much potential to show bad taste."

I suppose ties do add color if you happen to wear a conservative navy blue or black suit. In fact, nothing helps a two-year-old suit better than a new tie. What is it about a necktie that makes it the badge of formality or competence or authority? Linda Ellerbee said that, "If men can run the world, why can't they stop wearing neckties? How intelligent is it every morning to tie a noose around your neck?"

I've often wondered what the initial reason for wearing ties was. Did it serve some useful purpose at one time? For example, the buttons on the sleeves of men's suits were originally to keep the soldiers in Napoleon's army from wiping their noses on them; the buttons used to be big and rough. Were ties used like a bib to keep one from spilling food on a shirt? Now with the Internet at our fingertips, one can find all sorts of useless bits of information like this in just a few minutes.

Of course, some historical web sites implied a sexual symbolism of some sort. You'd be surprised to hear what is said about other aspects of clothing, such innocent things as pockets and codpieces. Clinton happened to wear a tie that Monica Lewinsky had given him on the very day that she began her testimony, and Ken Starr, paranoid as he was, suggested that Bill was trying to give her a signal. More likely, the president had so many ties that he couldn't remember who gave him which. If you notice, men in power, either in politics or business, all wear ties with little variability in the colors or the patterns. They are mostly striped, and blue and red are certainly more predominant than other colors. There are a lot of novelty ties, and most of them vie for attention with the ties that relatives give uncles or fathers-in-law for whom they can't think of a more personal or desired gift.

In the 1960's men rebelled against wearing ties as a result of the rebellion against tradition and the formality of dress, but the Nehru jackets and polyester leisure suits that were part of that same trend, went out of favor quickly, and ties became even more popular than ever. It's the rare man who can get away without wearing a tie - Nelson Mandela almost never wears a tie, saying he thinks it symbolizes a limit on freedom. I heard recently that the Dutch premier shed his tie in a grand gesture at a public function and that the entire country was doing it for awhile.

Of course it wasn't just ties that I thought were uncomfortable, but it was the tie clasps and tie tacks, as well. Then there were the different kinds of knots. I finally got so tired of fooling with ties that I bought some cheap clip-on ties at K-Mart. The only trouble with them was that they looked cheap and were always shorter than the usual tie and just looked really bad. But clip-ons were so comfortable to take off during the day when I could just do paperwork in my office and didn't have to be in meetings or committees or seeing patients.

I still kept getting my share of regular ties for Christmas and birthdays, though, and some were very nice and expensive, made out of pure silk. Then I got the idea to use the clip-on device from a cheap tie and put it on a regular tie that I had already tied into a Windsor knot; in fact, Ann became really good at doing this. The thing was never to let others know they were clip-on ties, because they somehow just didn't carry the authority or fashion sense that the regular tie did.

If I had more of a neck, or rather, less of a neck, and weighed about twenty-five pounds less, I'd have worn turtlenecks a lot of the time and given up those…ties that bind.

The Back of the Bus

I grew up in the segregated South. My family's only interaction with African Americans was as cheap labor, such as maids or yard men. They were referred to by genteel, *unprejudiced* white people as *Nigras*, or if you really wanted to be seen as *liberal,* as Negroes. Some people referred to them as colored. From a child's point of view, we seemed to treat them very well, although always from a viewpoint of the white person's helping them or giving them things. We had a woman who ironed clothes; she was paid a certain amount, given bus fare extra, and was provided a hot meal during the middle of the day. She was even allowed to sit in the breakfast room and eat dinner (not called lunch in the South in those days.) She always came in the back door, never the front. We always called her by her first name, Annie or Ella, and she in turn called all of us by our first names, although addressed my mother and grandmother by adding Mrs. to their first names—Mrs. Ruth and Mrs. Janie, although it was pronounced more like *Misserus.* We often gave her leftovers to take home with her.

Our yard man had eleven children, and he was given all the clothes I or my twin sisters had outgrown. We often provided pitchers of lemonade for him and however many of his children were helping on any particular day. In all of these interactions, though, it was clear which way the relationship went—master to servant, giver to receiver, high to low, better than thou to less fortunate. There really didn't appear to be any hostility or anger involved.

I never understood why African-Americans were treated as second-class citizens, though. I always felt offended somehow when *nigger* jokes were told. In fact, we were told that this was an offensive term and that we shouldn't use it and should use the more humane terms. Yet these same family members and friends saw no contradiction when they told *nigger* jokes.

During the 2nd World War, we rode the bus a lot because of the gasoline shortage. I had to go across town, transferring buses each Saturday to march at the Armory, as did all the school patrol boys. We were rewarded with free movie tickets to the first-run movies downtown. So I was on four different buses every Saturday. The back door of the bus marked the line in back of which the blacks could sit. White people, however, could sit anywhere on the bus and take all the seats, as far back at the last seat across the back, so that they wouldn't have to stand up. If blacks got on, they had to stand and in no way could they share a double seat or even a seat for four if a white person was sitting on it. This usually wasn't a problem except in the afternoon when all the black maids were returning to the poorest black section of town, and they outnumbered the number of seats behind the back door. They had to crowd into that area and stand up, even if there were plenty of seats on the front of the bus. The front of the bus actually meant the three-fourths of the seats in front of the back door.

After the war, when many more blacks were riding the buses than whites, this became more of a problem, but the blacks almost never crossed that line. If they did, often the white bus driver would just refuse to start the bus and would just sit there glaring into the back of the bus, often not saying anything. The blacks would then move to the back where they had to stand up. As I mentioned, it didn't work the other way. Whites, if more in number, would sit anywhere, and blacks had to stand even if there were plenty of seats farther up front, from passengers getting off, and the white people, somewhat defiantly, not moving up to take their vacated seats. Years later, in Tennessee, after the so-called civil rights movement had begun in earnest, I was sitting next to a black person and got up to give my seat to a pregnant white person. She wouldn't take my seat.

I think race relations is the one area where we've made the least progress. It was only after I settled in Indianapolis that I had co-workers, both professionals and those in more menial jobs, who were black. It was the first chance I had to associate with black people who were at the same socioeconomic level, or even higher, as the case may have been, as we had several black psychiatrists at the hospital as service chiefs, and one who later became Superintendent of the hospital. I was in a poker group of seven or eight that included a high school teacher (later to become a principal), an insurance salesman, a social worker, and sometimes a psychology intern who were all black. And yet at the start of my work here, I learned one day from one of the white psychiatrists that a study group of psychiatrists had held a late meeting and then adjourned to get something to eat around 7 PM at the Working Men's Friend, a tavern not far from the medical center. Since the group included a black woman psychiatrist, when they sat down, the waiters disappeared. It took the group awhile to figure out what was going on, but when they did, one psychiatrist went to the kitchen in search of a waiter, and was told that one of their group appeared to have had too much to drink, and thus they would not wait on them. It was segregation again and in an unusual place. The Workingmen's Friend at that time was filled with medical center personnel at lunch time, but in the evenings it became a typical blue collar red neck tavern. Needless to say, the place was boycotted by many at the medical center for several years until the place changed owners.

I always thought of the United States of America as a melting pot. Sure, many nationalities lived in conclaves with their own kind for awhile, the Irish, the Italians, etc. but eventually they all seemed to become acculturated and mixed in with all the other nationalities. I thought for awhile we would all truly become color blind. We truly wouldn't have to refer to people by their race anymore. We tried to teach our children not to use race when referring to people or to describe them, the same as one would not do with someone who was disabled. There are other ways to refer to people with polio residuals than crippled or people who had lost an eye as the one with a funny eye. Most of the time it's best to refer to people without regard to race, yet most still do it, mostly as a shorthand, but try it sometime and you'll begin to see how easy it can be.

I don't think people should be proud of their race or heritage or history or customs, etc. in the sense that they didn't choose their skin color, or their nationality - in fact, they had absolutely nothing to do with it; they had and have no control over it. It's another thing to choose to engage in certain celebrations or traditions, but if it is something over which you had no control, then you have no right to consider it other than something neutral - as a given.

A Wild Ride

Just when I started to relax and think that there were some helpful, good people in the world, the stranger who was driving started yelling and flailing his arms, and the car, going downhill now, started going faster and faster. What had we gotten ourselves into? Was he having an epileptic seizure? This Christian on his way home from church on Sunday morning was cursing a mile a minute and was doing eighty-five miles per hour at least. His wife grabbed the steering wheel, and he slowed down, then veered across the center line and slammed on the brakes just as we came face to face with the side of a mountain. Since a deep ravine was on the other side, I suppose I felt somewhat relieved.

It had started off well - we had just bought a new car for our vacation and we'd had a good time in Florida. We were on our way back home, taking a different route so that we could also stop by to see Ann's parents in Virginia for a visit. We'd had a Sunday buffet breakfast at the motel and were on our way through North Carolina when suddenly, going up a hill, the car started to overheat. I couldn't believe this - a new car and something already wrong with it. Then the car stopped, just around a curve almost at the top of the hill. We all got out, and Ann went back around the curve to warn people a stalled car was ahead. The kids and I pushed the car over to the side where there was just enough room so that none of it stuck out into the road. The heat was stifling with no breeze at all, one of those days when your clothes stick to you like Saran wrap. All the antifreeze had leaked out and the car wouldn't start. I then went around the curve to see if I could flag down someone.

An older model station wagon, with a man, woman, and little girl stopped, and they asked if they could help. We noticed that the man had a cast on his left arm. We asked if they knew where the nearest filling station was, and they told us it was just on the other side of the hill, and to hop in and they'd take us there. There said they were on their way home from church. That's when our wild ride began.

As we finally came to stop, inches away from the side of the hill, the man jumped out and flung his arm with the cast up and down. He said a bee had gotten under his cast and stung him and that he was allergic to bees. He told us that his arm was already beginning to swell. His wife took the wheel as we all jumped back into the car. We thanked them as they let us off at the station, and they proceeded on their way to the hospital emergency room. We were just grateful that our wild ride had ended.

Goodbye, R2D2 or Whatever

My mother married for the second time the same year that Ann and I were married - 1960. She and Carey had both been married before, and each had three grown children. I had met Ginger, Carey's oldest daughter, years before, but certainly didn't know her well. The fact that I was in graduate school at Vanderbilt and that Ann and I lived in Nashville, then moved here to Indianapolis in 1961 kept us from getting to know Carey and his extended family well. For some reason, Ginger drove through Indianapolis on her way back to her teaching job in Colorado Springs in 1963 and spent a day or two with us. She was pleasant, but we didn't seem to have much in common, really, except my mother and her father.

We visited mother and Carey about once a year for many, many years; but our vacations never coincided with Ginger's, who in time married an older divorced man who had four children. Ginger and Forrest then proceeded to have three children of their own, for a total of seven children. Since Forrest's children were older, they were soon getting to the age where they were marrying and starting families of their own. We had always exchanged Christmas cards and then about thirty years ago, Ginger started sending us a Christmas newsletter. We had trouble knowing who was who but weren't concerned about it much because we never saw them. In fact, the only time I met Forrest and the last time I saw Ginger was at Carey's funeral, which occurred in 1981. I never met any of her children or stepchildren.

Through the years we laughed because the mimeographed (remember the purple ink?) letters read like the goings-on of the most perfect family that ever lived on the face of the earth. Each year the letter got longer and longer; first from a Selectric typewriter and then from a personal computer, and then in a font made so small one could barely make it out. The worst thing, though, was that probably because the letter went to so many people who didn't know the family members, she referred to their combined seven children with numbers from one to seven, and then to their offspring with the letters of the alphabet, 1A for 1's first child, 1B for the second child, etc. and then to *their* offspring with another number, so that you heard about Roxy

(1) and her daughter as 1A, and then her daughter's daughter as 1A1 , sort of like the steak sauce. And so on down the evolutionary line, 2, 2A, 2A1, etc. After a few years of this saccharine newsletter arriving every Christmas with no other news and not even a personalized signature, and after my mother's death, we stopped reciprocating with even a card. Nevertheless, the newsletters kept coming, with smaller and smaller print and more and more grandiose paragraphs about each family member. I would include here some quotes, but the information was so far removed from our lives that we didn't bother keeping them.

I remembered once reading in Ann Landers's column, of a very sarcastic response being made by a reader who had become fed up with such literary missives and made up one of her own. It started out with the husband being passed up for a promotion, getting mad and quitting his job, her oldest son being defeated for home room monitor and flunking French - well, you get the idea. I'd often thought of sending this column to Ginger. Now don't get me wrong, I'm not talking about newsletters from close friends or relatives where you know and love all the people concerned and are eager to hear about their activities and experiences. I'm talking about people we've never met, most probably never will, and who never put in a personal word or from whom we never hear during the rest of the entire year.

This past season Ann Landers again published the sarcastic newsletter, and I clipped it out and thought of sending it to Ginger anonymously. But, I could never do anything of that sort anonymously. I thought of sending it with a clever letter, asking about 1A4 and 3B2, but then this year I didn't get the infamous newsletter by Christmas and I thought, "Aha! they have either gotten the message, died, or - ," and then on December 27th the family newsletter arrived, telling about their travels to Europe, their new family members, and their prizes and accomplishments, and I thought, "Okay, this year I'm going to send them an answer they won't soon forget." The only reason I had hesitated before or had been ambivalent was that I thought the best way to extinguish this behavior was to ignore them completely, not responding in any way at all. Obviously, this hadn't worked. But then I read the last couple of paragraphs and thought, for the first time ever, what a beautiful Christmas message their newsletter would have been if they had included just that one small section.

They wrote about visiting a B&B in Scotland called Monday's Cottage. The woman who owned it claimed that Monday was her favorite day of the week because every Monday was a new beginning. The woman had been widowed and had worked hard all her life, raising three children, but she borrowed money to convert the cottage into a B&B to supplement her retirement income. They said it made them reflect on their own lives and wished all many Mondays.

I guess I've had a change of heart. Maybe I'll just keep these thoughts to myself or write about them for the memoir writing group and not send any response at all. Maybe I am more of an optimist that I thought, and maybe they'll write again next year about another interesting person they've met, rather than only themselves.

Postscript (Christmas, 2007) The annual newsletter arrived; alas, more news of themselves and their accomplishments, but also news of deaths, diseases, treatments - more like real life. There were no interesting stories of anyone outside the family. Oh, well - maybe it's the thought that counts - now that's a scary view!

Buried, But Not Gone

In Oak Ridge, Tennessee, locked in a lead box in the middle of a concrete slab, buried far underground, covered with more concrete, is the probable cause of Ann's leukemia. That was the fate of the radium that seventeen student nurses and numerous other nursing and hospital staff had taken from patients and transferred to a metal box on an upper floor of Rutherford Hospital. We learned this at a breakfast arranged by Dolly Cordell, a former nursing school classmate of Ann's. She had just retired the day before, and her retirement had been the impetus for the graduating class of 1955's 45th reunion.

The nursing students hadn't used any protection except for rubber gloves, yet the effects of handling even small amounts of radium had been documented decades earlier when many women in upper state New York who had painted glow-in-the-dark watch faces developed various forms of cancer at a rate much higher than the average woman their age. Of seventeen former nursing students, one had already died from cancer and one had been too ill to attend a reunion. Six of the fifteen who attended had had or currently had cancer, one of them leukemia and then non-Hodgkin's lymphoma, just like Ann. Several others had immune system disorders.

One of the characteristics of the nurses who graduated from the Rutherford School of Nursing's program was professionalism, which included in that day and time and place, an unstated but strong warning not to question anything told them by a physician. Certainly, no one questioned procedures that she had been taught for treating cancer patients with radium - radium that had been bought and given to the hospital by a former patients's wealthy spouse years and years before.

The hospital and the affiliated school of nursing were steeped in tradition and professionalism, as well as the latest treatments of the day, especially for a small hospital in the mountains of North Carolina, half-way between Asheville and Charlotte. It was a town no one much has heard about, although there are other towns nearby that one has heard about as vacation spots for those who could afford a cottage in the mountains - such as Hendersonville or Lake

Lure, or for summer tourists the close-by town of Gatlinburg, Tennessee, even though in another state.

To get to the little town of Rutherfordton from Asheville, there appeared to be three routes from which to choose. Two involved interstates the whole way and one, which looked more scenic, was a combination of state roads, and this was the one we chose. The route wound through, around, over, and up a series of mountains, with hairpin curves and signs that told drivers to beware of falling rock, but the route was full of flowering trees - dogwoods, redbuds, pear trees - and wisteria vines growing on trees that hadn't blossomed yet themselves, so that they looked like "wisteria trees", and lots and lots of azaleas - pink, lavender, white, and salmon-colored. The rhododendron hadn't bloomed yet, but its green leaves were evident.

On the road, the fog was thick, not as bad as it had been on the Interstate, though. Since there was no nice inn or large motel in Rutherfordton, we checked into the Forest Inn, which sat on a small hill overlooking the nearby town of Forest City. We turned on the TV and got caught up in the news, which was all about the case of Elian Gonzalez. Then there was a national CNN news broadcast interruption telling about a 100-car pile-up on U.S. 40 near Black Mountain, close to the place we turned off onto a little side road - probably not more than twenty-five miles from the huge pile-up where two motorists were killed, at least fifteen injured, and scores of cars damaged. The cars shown in the images on TV had been compacted like soda cans.

The trip to Rutherfordton was planned with anticipation, but also anxiety - anxiety at what Ann might find out about the people affected by the radium. There was a slight anxiety hovering over me, as well, as we had planned to write about the trip for our memoirs group, each from our own perspective, without comparing notes. Since I'd met only three of her former classmates a few years before, very briefly, I had Ann tell me a little about each woman. The names were confusing because they had all been referred to by their last names while in nursing school - their maiden names. It turned out that all but one had married, so I had to learn their new last names as well as their first names. I wondered - would the people who did or said the things Ann had told me about be, in any way, the same now? Surely, forty-five years would have made a difference. Would the one who was clumsy and fell all the time still be clumsy and would she fall? (Yes, she had fallen just two days prior to the reunion and broken two ribs.) Would the flirt, the girl whom all the others would never leave alone with their boyfriends in the living room of the nursing school residence, still be a flirt? (Yes, she came without her husband and flirted with many of the other men present.)

The night before the main day's events, at dinner with a couple of old nursing school friends and their relatives, I heard lots of anecdotes and stories

- being elaborated on, changed, contradicted, or even denied as happening at all. Even the next day when we checked the stories with the others, more versions were added rather than getting a definite clarification. Was it really Ann who, very early in the first year, was asked by a senior nursing student, to go get a Fallopian tube? Three agreed, one said the incident occurred, but it wasn't Ann, although it was a common joke played on new students, and Ann swears she would have remembered such an incident if indeed it had been she.

When Ann and I returned from a trip or even after a few hours of being away and checked the answering machine, I always said, if there were no messages, "Nobody loves us", and she always said, "No news is good news", or wait, was Ann the one who said, "Nobody loves us", and I the one who said …

Wapihani I

I've always loved being around water - the ocean, a lake, a river, even a pond. At one point in my life, I realized that I was probably going to spend the rest of my life in the Midwest, far from the ocean. I didn't think we could move to a home on a river or a lake, so I decided to do what I could afford at the time. I bought a flat-bottomed aluminum row boat and some oars. I spent a lot of time thinking about names for the boat, not that the boat was the type to have a name, particularly, but because I wanted it to be symbolic. I was hoping, you see, to have another boat one day and call it the Wapihani II, so I called this one the Wapihani I. Wapihani means White River, and I think I ran across this little piece of information while visiting Conner Prairie Farm - a historic site just north of Indianapolis.

I thought that the kids would like to go boating, and they went out a couple of times, but then they didn't want to go anymore. It was too boring and uneventful. It was too much trouble to row. It was too much trouble to haul around to a river and to get it actually in the water. I bought some heavy, ready-made rubber pieces, four of them, that went under the four corners of the boat, but you had to lift the boat up on the top of the car, and, of course, do it very carefully, so that you wouldn't scratch the car. It took two people - one person couldn't do it, because it was both too heavy and too awkward. But with two people, it wasn't really that difficult, and the weight of the boat caused the rubber pieces to stay on the car by suction.

One day when the kids had other more interesting things to do, Ann and I took the boat up to 86th St., just east of Keystone Ave. and drove under the bridge and parked the car. This was before the mall, Keystone at the Crossing, was built there, and 86th St. was only two lanes then. We put the boat in the river. We'd read that the river flowed south, and we'd already parked Ann's car at Broad Ripple Park, which is where we thought we'd end up. It was a beautiful, clear, hot summer day, and we planned to be on the river for several hours. We saw a lot of wildlife - turtles that would jump off rocks where they had been sunning themselves, and muskrats, blue herons, and squirrels as we passed by. Occasionally, a fish would jump up not far from the boat.

The river was actually very shallow in many places because it hadn't rained in a while. There was very little traffic on the river, and the trees were still leafy enough that you couldn't see much of the shore, except where there were houses with sloping lawns down to the river. We didn't know just how much the river twisted and turned, and the flow of the river didn't actually help us much. In fact, we had to row pretty constantly to make any headway. It took a lot longer than we had thought. Every so often a small speedboat would come along and the waves from them would almost tip us over, but we learned to turn the boat to face the waves and not let the waves catch us sideways.

It was pretty warm, and the drinks in the cooler were gone in an hour or so. There wasn't any dock or landing to get your boat out of the water in Broad Ripple Park either as there is now, but for quite a while we just drifted down the lazy river, and it was one of the most relaxing days we've ever spent. We thought of doing it again sometime, but for one reason or another, we never did.

We sold the boat in a garage sale not too long after that. An older man bought it, he said, to take his grandchildren fishing. I wished him luck! I had thought about removing all the letters spelling Wapihani, but then I thought no, I'd leave them on, and maybe someday we'd see the Wapihani I as we passed it in the Wapihani II.

Road Mapped, Tattooed, and Zapped

When the doctor told Ann that he thought she should have a series of radiation treatments, we didn't know what she was in for. But after having several different kinds of chemotherapy and a new monoclonal antibody therapy, radiation didn't sound so bad, or at least not any worse that the previous treatments. From talking with a few other friends and acquaintances, we knew the treatments had to be delivered in a hospital setting, but all said that they were painless, except for the tattooing and maybe a few side effects.

Ann's ordeal began when she met the new radiation oncologist, who, for the very first time, showed us pictures of the lymphoma, not just one, but an entire series taken from the CAT Scan. Ann and I could see for the first time just what was causing her all this trouble. There sat the lymphoma, or tumor, or bunch of clustered lymph nodes right in the middle of her abdomen, not really pressing on anything - between the kidneys, between the liver and the spleen, almost dead center. He said that radiation isn't usually used for lymphoma, but hers was such a distinct conglomerate, that he thought a series of doses aimed very precisely at the lymphoma would shrink it greatly, if not do away with it entirely. How could one resist his recommendations, with such a good explanation and prognosis? He was willing to answer any and all questions and even had a nice bedside manner, very personable and with a sense of humor. In the middle of her exam, he looked over to me and asked, "Been to Key West lately?" I didn't get his drift at first, until he said, "...for the Hemingway look-alike contest?"

Shortly thereafter, Ann was given a series of appointments to be measured for the treatments. When I say road mapped, that is exactly what her abdomen looked like, with red and blue wavy lines that did indeed resemble a map, with the bunches of dots looking like cities and towns. At first we thought this was the tattooing we had heard about, but that was to come later, after she had already had a couple of treatments. A big needle was used to make very discrete marks, and she was told she could now wash away all the red and blue lines, as these dots were permanent, or unable to be washed away in any ordinary bathing.

At Ann's first actual treatment we were greeted in the waiting room by a volunteer, who turned out to be a former child psychologist at Riley Hospital, and whom I had known for many years. She's retired now, too, and does volunteer work twice a week at St. Vincent Hospital. It turns out that she had breast cancer and underwent the same type of radiation that Ann would have, so she was a good source of information, as well as being an example of hope, since she had beat the cancer that afflicted her several years earlier.

Do Actions Always Speak Louder Than Words?

After the memoirs group two weeks ago, Ann had gone out to the parking lot to get some books from the car's trunk for Court and Barb, our best friends and also members of the memoir group, when a woman called to her from the far north side of the lot. The woman started walking over to Ann, and Ann went to meet her. She asked if Ann could tell her how to get to Arlington Avenue. Ann, as usual, knew it was nearby but hadn't a clue as to how to direct someone there. Meanwhile, the woman was saying that she had gotten lost on a walk - got all mixed up, but if Ann could just point out the way to Arlington, she could find her way home. She said she was supposed to be out for a walk, because the doctor had said she needed to walk because of her heart, but now she was feeling ill, besides being lost. She offered to pay Ann if she would just drive her home. Ann confessed to her that she wasn't as familiar with this section of town, but that she'd go in and get her husband to drive them, and she told the woman to sit in the shade and she'd be right back.

Ann came in and told me the bare essentials of this scenario, and then inquired of the group what else could she do? I, meantime, had pictured an elderly, confused woman out for a walk, who had maybe gotten too warm in the almost 80-degree temperature. I was therefore somewhat surprised to see a black woman whose age I'd estimate as in her middle thirties in no obvious distress, not appearing hot nor bothered, approaching the entrance to the church lobby. I inquired about her health, and she again repeated that she had heart problems and was out walking, as she usually did, but had come from a different direction, pointing to the south end of the parking lot and mentioning a street that I knew was in that direction. She then asked if this building wasn't a school; when we replied that it was a church, she said, "Wasn't Cathedral around here somewhere?", evidently referring to the high school a good ways down the street. Was this confusion?

What struck me about the woman was how young she looked in terms of my expectations and the fact that she didn't look ill - not out of breath or sweating. In fact, her make-up and hair and general demeanor gave no hint of confusion, nor even anxiety. Going into psychiatric jargon, her affect appeared to be flat. I asked if she lived nearby and where she wanted to go. She said, "...home", and if Arlington was right there, in the direction I had just pointed, she said that she lived "...just off Arlington, at 6051 Laurel Hall Drive." I again asked her if she felt sick - I could imagine her collapsing in my car, or worse yet, throwing up inside the car. But after looking at her more carefully, I discarded these notions and thought of fantasies of her taking Ann and me to a house or apartment where a couple of accomplices would be lying in wait to rob us. I noticed that she used good grammar and also that her long, painted red fingernails looked as though they had been manicured by a professional.

When we got to the car, Ann opened the front door for her to get in, saying that she would sit in the back, so that the woman could take advantage of the air-conditioning that maybe would revive this person who looked as if she needed no reviving. She seemed slightly uncomfortable that she would be in the front seat, with Ann sitting directly behind her. I told her, only half-jokingly, that she looked too young to have heart trouble, and she responded that all her family had heart problems. I pointed to 56th Street and told her that Arlington was the next street east. She said, all at once, without stopping, to take a right onto Arlington, and then go to Laurel Hall Drive, which would be off to the left. When we turned onto Arlington, she immediately told me to get in the left lane because I needed to turn left in about three more blocks; again her directions were pretty specific.

As I turned left on Laurel Hall Drive, I immediately noticed that a sign said, "Not a Thru Street," and I wondered if she would direct me to the last house on the block. When I asked which side of the street she lived on, she said the right side, and said it was an apartment building, but didn't give a number. She really did look at this point as though she were having trouble deciding which apartment building it was, even though there were only two on the block, most of the houses being single-family dwellings. I asked her if there would be someone at home, and she replied, "Yes." She didn't say whom or give any further details. She never gave us her name.

I pulled up front, avoiding the long driveway leading to the rear of the building, and she hurriedly got the door open, thanked us, and walked up to the entrance and inside, without a glance backward.

I didn't notice that she had been clutching a large handbag, which Ann said she had noticed earlier and had wondered why someone going out on a walk would have brought it along, rather than just a key.

Looking back, I wonder if she had had any uneasy thoughts about Ann and me robbing her. I doubt that - that is probably my imagination working overtime.

While all this was going on I couldn't help but wonder if Ann (or both of us) had been the intended victims of a robbery or car theft. Did the woman really live at 6051 Laurel Hall Drive or had she picked out the apartment building because she would have no trouble getting inside or to her accomplices? Would she have faked fainting or dizziness to get us to help her inside the building or up the stairs? She certainly wasted no time getting from the car into the building, and without a backward glance.

Would we have thought these same thoughts if the woman had been white or Hispanic, whether she'd been much older or in more obvious distress?

When Ann had come back to get me, a few in the memoirs group also appeared slightly suspicious. Chuck even offered to go with us, and Jane ran out to the car wondering if we were doing the right thing?

What would the right thing have been, under the circumstances? Should we have asked for some identification? That seems logical now, particularly if it had a Laurel Hall address on it. Or should we have offered to call relatives at home for her?

Eyewitness reports are known for their inaccuracy, and the inaccuracy gets larger and larger as time goes on. That's why I wrote all of this down, right after lunch on the day it occurred.

Isn't it a sad state of affairs if everything had been on the up-and-up - 100 per cent truthful, and yet we somehow felt we'd been taken advantage of?

Could it be feasible that our worst fears had been true, but that the woman lost her nerve, or thought maybe there'd been too many witnesses and decided to pull this scam another time at another place?

Or could it have been that again our views were correct, but she also thought that maybe there still were helpful people in the world and that our actions were not stupid and gullible, but showed just a slight trace of compassion and empathy for a fellow being? I don't think so.

Who knows? Do our actions really speak louder than our unuttered words? Was it all true, and were we just being overly cautious? Were we racial stereotyping? Will we ever find out?

Fault Lines

I've got a lot of faults. I'm not the first to admit that - a lot of people have told me so - in so many words.

I'm fat. I eat as though I'm feeding an angry mob down in my stomach, and I've got to hurry and throw food down to it to quell the disturbance.

I'm also sarcastic. Most of the time I call it a sense of humor, but I recognize it for what it is - sarcasm.

I procrastinate, too. I have to think about things before doing them. I have to weigh the pros and cons - what would the consequences be of this or that? My priorities are mixed up. I always do the most important things last. My reasoning is if I get all the little things done and out of the way, then I'll have the time and effort to devote to the really important things. Of course, I always find more *little* things to do, and by the time I'm through with all of them, then I'm too tired or it's too late to deal with the necessary things.

Sometimes I'm envious and I covet. I could easily be even more materialistic that I already am.

These are just some of my faults. Now I could start to describe my good qualities, and I'm sure they would outnumber and outweigh my faults, but I'd probably just be getting myself off the hook. After all, surely I can list more than one typewritten page of faults or I could list some traits that people would list when they really want to avoid divulging anything about themselves. These are usually such traits as perfectionism or ruthless honesty or competitiveness - things one can admit to and still feel superior or smug or holier than thou. In fact, a lot of times the traits you put in one column as desirable could as easily be put in the undesirable column.

I'm vain. Sometimes I whine, and I hate that. I hate whiners and whining.

I like to throw things up to people. I love to *catch* someone in a mistake. I love to say, "I told you so." I try not to do these things but I don't always succeed.

I'm selfish and certainly overly-critical - and Ann says I'm mean.

Say it isn't so.

The Rook Game

I couldn't believe what was going on under the table. Janet, it seemed, was brushing her leg up against mine. Well, not exactly brushing her leg against mine as lightly kicking me. It seemed so unlikely that I thought I must be imagining it, considering with whom we were playing Rook. Then, we made eye contact, which I'd been trying to avoid for several minutes. She was trying to tell me something - trying to *cheat,* for God's sake. *Janet* - I couldn't believe it. It would have been almost more believable if she had been trying to flirt with me, but cheating? It turned out that the Petersons thought cheating at Rook was what everyone did, even Christians like them - just good-natured fun. Cheating at cards was so inconsequential that it was in a category with telling white lies, such as telling a relative that you like her dress or new hairdo or the horrible wallpaper that's just been used in the family room. It wasn't like poker, where money was involved, or bridge, where everyone was so serious. Of course, Rook is played with a special deck of cards and is sometimes referred to as "missionary poker" or "Christian cards."

Janet and Bill Peterson had been our neighbors for several years. Just before they moved in, Marie, our friend across the street, right next door to them, said she hoped that it would be a fun couple. Well, they just were not the kind of people you could describe as a fun couple in the 1960's. They were, however, hard-working, church-attending people who turned out to be good neighbors. But we didn't have so much in common that we continued to be friends after we moved to a different neighborhood. For several years after we moved, we would occasionally run into them, usually at a cafeteria or a supermarket, because they, too, had moved.

When bumping into Janet the other day at the new Marsh Supermarket, I learned that Bill still worked at the company where they started each day with a prayer, and that Janet taught at a religious school, but they were planning retirement soon. I wondered if their lives were any different and if they ever played Rook with their neighbors.

Just a Sun Spot

I was surprised that it was such a large box. It looked about as big as a woman's hat box. I was surprised even more when he handed it to me and I almost dropped it, thinking it would be light as a hat box - more like a box of oatmeal. When I finally had it securely in my hands, it was quite heavy and filled with solid pieces that I could rattle around. When I looked at him questioningly, he said they were bone fragments.

Most of my knowledge of cremation and ashes came from old movies, where the cremated remains of people were always in small ornamental vases or urns that people opened to the breeze on bridges or dusted from airplanes or large ships at sea, or finally placed on mantels above fireplaces.

When Margaret died, it was wintertime in Indiana and cold and snowy. She had requested cremation, so we decided to have her body cremated and to take her remains back to Virginia to be buried next to her husband. Now in the tiny hamlet of St. Paul, Virginia, out of hundreds and hundreds of people, only three people who had been cremated were buried in the cemetery in the mountains just outside of town. I thought it was as if people didn't believe in double jeopardy, not seeing the need to be done away with twice, but it instead seems to be more an attitude against cremation - based on religious beliefs.

On the trip to Virginia the next May, I kiddingly told friends at work that I was going to put a bumper sticker on the car that said, "Mother-in-law in trunk." People always acted shocked, as if I were somehow being cruel or unfeeling, whereas I know Margaret would have gotten a laugh out of it. She had a keen sense of humor, and we had kidded back and forth a lot.

We had arranged for the cemetery workers to have a hole dug in the ground next to where her husband lay buried, just in front of the huge rock Ann's sister Helen had had placed there like a large boulder - rough and unpolished unlike most of the other tombstones. I was thinking that the hole would be about a couple of feet deep at the most, but when we got there, it looked a good six to eight feet deep and about a foot square.

Ann and Helen wanted to shovel some of the mound of dirt from the large heap nearby, but the workers misunderstood, and we ended up shoveling all the dirt in, while the workers left and stood quite a distance away from us. I couldn't tell if they just wanted to disassociate themselves from us or from the cremated remains so unusual to them.

Just before we left, I got out my camera and took some photographs of the gravesite, the stone, and surroundings. The sun had come out and was shining full force by this time. One of the photographs later startled us when we got it back from being developed. A stream of light reflected off the boulder as it reached into the sky. What was that - some indication of Margaret's soul going to heaven? That was the first thought, of course, but then we realized that it was just a sun spot on the lens, however interesting other explanations might be.

Human Nature

I wonder what's different about human nature at the Sea View Inn on Pawley's Island, S.C. Aren't people the same everywhere? The answer, of course, is no - they aren't. Expectations can strongly influence human behavior. The Sea View Inn has no keys to any of the rooms, no locks on any of the doors, unless you count the little latches on the bathroom doors. No one seems to worry that something - a piece of jewelry, a wallet with credit cards, money, a camera - might be stolen. Perhaps no one has the need, as most of the guests appear to be fairly well off, although you wouldn't necessarily know that from the way they dress - sort of shabby-chic beach clothes, often going barefoot, or in flip-flops or well-worn sandals.

No television sets or telephones distract at Sea View, and cell phones were not allowed just a few years ago; no *USA Todays* cover the tables in the large great room.

Guests sit at assigned tables in the dining room. The tables are usually set with water or sweetened iced tea and some appetizer, such as strips of ham and freshly-sliced pears or just-cooked sweet potato chips. The main course is brought in to all thirty-six diners within the first two or three minutes. The servers bring out huge casseroles or platters of food and serve each table individually. Bowls of vegetables are placed on each table. The servers are piqued if you only eat half a dessert or fail to sample one of the dishes. Staff clears the tables rapidly as guests anticipate the eagerly-awaited desserts that are served with each and every meal. The food is healthy and the meals are always well-balanced.

Paintings from the watercolor workshop held each spring decorate the inn. Many of the paintings are of the inn or some part of it, such as the long porch with tall-backed rocking chairs and two big hammocks. On the rear enclosed porch is a long row of brightly-colored director chairs, a refrigerator for guests' bottles of wine or soft drinks, and a large liquor cabinet with guests' bottles labeled with their names, and with lemons and limes and clear plastic wine goblets. In the morning, before breakfast, there's a long table with cups and saucers and pots of coffee or hot water for a variety of spiced teas.

In the main room, on a large antique secretary, there's a five-year guest book, where guests have signed in, giving their names and addresses. Besides a lot of towns and cities across the entire continental U.S., guests from Alaska, Germany, Greece, S. Africa, Mexico, and Canada are listed just during the past twelve months. About ten large photo albums contain not only earlier pictures of the inn and its current owners, but photographs taken by guests staying there who then sent them back for inclusion in albums.

A library of books that guests are allowed to read without signing any little index cards or list is very inviting, and you may take the book back home with you, with the understanding that you'll mail it back when you've finished reading it.

There're also cabinets with games and cards. A lot of people sit around reading in the great room, on one of the porches, or out on a deck half-way from the house to the beach, or even on the beach; but just as many sit either talking or just staring out at the ocean waves or the beach or the flag that seems to be always blowing in the wind. At night sometimes there are people with flashlights walking along in pairs or small groups on the beach.

After dinner, talking is more animated, and occasionally discussions spring up that involve the entire group in any one place, usually the great room. Almost never are the discussions about current events, but more about previous visits to Pawley's Island, or books, or philosophical issues, or things that make people laugh - rarely jokes, but just funny events or stories.

A few *rules* indicate that no guests are allowed for meals unless notice is given at least twenty-four hours in advance. This rule is followed strictly, even though some of the others, such as no one in a bathing suit is allowed in the great room, are often overlooked. No one is *ever* allowed in the kitchen, even for an instant, and if you open the door, someone will talk to you but escort you out while doing so. If a guest remarks how good a dish is, a server will always give a thank-you, but if ever asked about the ingredients, will only enumerate a few and will often add, "...and some other things." If a guest appears to be interested in a recipe, she is almost admonished, saying that Page, the owner, is responsible for the menus and makes all the recipes and that she would never give a recipe away, hinting that the cooks and kitchen staff would never think of revealing any of Page's "secret" recipes.

The furnishings appear to be a mish-mash of wicker, antiques, Amish or Amish-inspired simple, utilitarian tables, some obviously hand-crafted. There are lots of overhead fans, but no air-conditioning in the main house, except for the office, which must be cooled because of the computers. Sea shells, oil lamps, mismatched lamps, and a large fireplace and mantel are at one end. The dining room is kept closed until the meals are announced by a melody played on three large dinner bells, after which the two wide doors to the dining room are swung open to all the guests who are eagerly awaiting the appointed hour. The salt air seems to increase one's appetite mysteriously, and while guests frequently carry around bottles of water or soft drinks, or coffee or wine, only very young children ever resort to a snack between meals, even late into the evening.

There seems to be a breeze most of the time, and it's usually quite welcome as the temperature hovers in the middle eighties to low nineties in the summer.

It's nice to go back to a place that is essentially the same year after year - for many years. The art work may change, the upholstery of the same couches and chairs, but the traditions and little practices seem almost written in stone, which is comforting for people coming back after thirty years, especially children whose parents brought them in the first place and who are now bringing their own children.

There was a change, however, from when we had last been there, almost five years before. Frances, the head server, on Wednesday evening, spoke in a voice we could all hear. She was staring at the people at the largest table - maybe ten of them, saying they had been noisy, but they were okay now - tonight. She then walked to the table for four next to them and said that table was nice, and then the next table of two, she said was quiet. Then, as if it hadn't been planned, she burst into song in this booming, operatic, church choir-voice, singing, "May God bless you." It seemed totally out of character. She kept on singing just that one phrase in all kinds of melodies and vocal ranges - as if someone had turned the television on to a Gospel station as loud as you could get it. People put down their silverware and glasses, transfixed by her. It seems this was a fairly new part of the experience of staying there and was done on the last night of the week - usually a Friday, but she was leaving to go on a vacation the next morning to the Bronx where she was from, so instead of just not having this performance at all, she decided to include it earlier in the week, perhaps at the urging of someone who had witnessed it in recent years. It was the highlight of a memorable visit. You just can't predict human nature.

Double Trouble

When you have twin sisters, there's double trouble. This is as true when they are sixty-two as it was when they were six, twelve, or sixteen. Both of my sisters and their husbands and Ann and I got together recently at a cabin in the Poconos that one of my sisters owns. It was the first time we had all six been together for quite a number of years. Each of my sisters wanted to be the center of attention, trying to "one-up" the other, if the other seemed to be getting laughs with her reminiscences or family anecdotes. One way they tried to do this was to talk louder and louder, and can they talk loud!

My mother didn't know she was going to have twins, as her doctor could only hear one heartbeat, so she was quite surprised one day in 1938. She had one name picked out but then she decided that she needed to get both grandmothers' names and hers in the combinations because she said she wasn't going to have any more children. She finally decided on Margaret Ruth and Marjorie Jane. Ruth was Mother's name and the two grandmothers first names were Margaret and Jane; Marjorie was chosen because it sounded a lot like Margaret, she thought. Needless to say, instead of being called Margaret and Marjorie, the twins were always referred to as Peggy and Jane - so much for the three days it took to decide what to call them.

I was not quite four years old when they were born and don't remember much about it, except that a lot of formula had to be prepared, and there always seemed to be a fuss about getting matching outfits for them. Mother decided it would be cute to dress them alike. I can remember nightly arguments when they were older and in high school. They never deviated more than occasionally one's wearing a slightly different color or shade of blouse. No matter how long the arguments became, Peggy always won and Jane always gave in. I sometimes tried to put in my two cents' worth and would make suggestions. Whatever I suggested they always decided differently, even if I sided with one of them. They stuck together no matter what. They might decide on a Tuesday night that each would wear what each wanted on Wednesday morning, but when Wednesday morning came, it was always

Jane who gave in. I don't know why my mother didn't intervene - or maybe she did and they just ignored her suggestions, too.

It was interesting to see that after forty years this was no longer the case. Jane wanted to make as many of the decisions as possible - what kind of restaurant to go to, what to do next, who was going to ride in what car, etc.

I mentioned the writing group and even read them a couple of my memoirs. Of course, they remembered things differently from me, or it seemed didn't remember anything that I thought they would have remembered. It seemed unlikely that all three of us had grown up in the same household.

I never had any trouble telling them apart, even though they are supposedly identical twins. Sometimes, especially from a distance or when they were turned sideways, my mother and grandmother would get them mixed up. I never did. When they were seniors in high school, they traded dates and went on a double date and only told their dates who was really who at the end of the evening. Needless to say, neither boy ever dated them again.

Some school official had decided before enrolling them in first grade that they should be separated. I'd like to think that it was some forward-looking principal making this decision based on educational theory about the individuality of twins, but I think it was only because she thought that a first grade teacher would be unable to tell them apart.

Peggy and Jane dressed alike for eighteen years, even graduating from high school and attending the senior prom wearing identical dresses. They were married two years apart, but each wore the same wedding dress.

They had somewhat different interests in school - one was very interested and good in art and drawing, while the other seemed to have no particular abilities in this area. One was much more proficient in typing, for example, while the other didn't type as well. They both made good grades, always A's and B's, so it was hard to know if they really had different abilities or just different interests.

When our daughter was born, she received identical outfits from each - one from Jacksonville, Florida and one from West Lafayette, Indiana, although they were different colors. They hadn't conferred with each other about the gifts, either. I frequently got identical birthday cards from them through the years, as one continued to live in Florida, and the other had moved to Philadelphia.

Through the years, they had many of the same ailments - allergy problems, lots of difficulty with imbedded wisdom teeth, gall bladder operations, and even hysterectomies, all at roughly the same time.

Jane became involved in politics and was elected to the town board of commissioners and went into real estate, while the other took early retirement from Southern Bell, where she had worked since she was eighteen. She soon went back to work for a mortgage company, doing training and personnel work, much as she had done at the telephone company.

Telling one of them something, I finally learned, was like telling both of them, and while we never had any secrets, they always communicated with each other about everything.

In our conversations at the cabin, we learned that each of them has wondered if they were really identical, in terms of genetic make-up or not. Years ago, they learned that Mother had never questioned the obstetrician and had always just assumed they were identical because of how alike they looked. They even thought they'd investigate what tests would have to be performed to determine this, and one brother-in-law suggested they do something this summer, when they get together in Florida. The twins were double trouble, and I'm making odds of a million to one that they really are identical. No two could be so alike with just environment in common.

False Starts

Waiting - once you're conceived, you have to wait nine months to be born. You start out waiting and you end up waiting. I hate waiting because I think I could be doing something else - something constructive, maybe; something that needs to be done. Time spent waiting is time wasted. BLOCK. WRITER'S BLOCK! I can't think of anything else on this subject. No, wait. Maybe I could write about waiting rooms - one of the medical establishment's few aptly-named.........what? BLOCK. Nothing. Maybe I'll try a new subject.

Movies - I like to go to the movies, but going to the movies is strange. You stand in a line to get a ticket to sit in the dark with other people in a large auditorium. Being in a dark movie theater with lots of other people whom you don't know seems to help set the mood. It's sort of a feeling of, "We're all in this together, alone," to quote Lily Tomlin. BLOCK. WRITER'S BLOCK! I'll start again.

Bored on the Board - There's a joke that goes: Once a man went to his doctor for a check-up, and when he was finished, he sat across from the doctor's desk, and the doctor said, "I'm going to be honest with you. You've only got a year to live." The man couldn't believe his ears, so he asked the doctor again, only to hear the same thing repeated. Then, he asked the doctor what he should do, and the doctor looked very serious, leaned over and asked him, "Don't you live in a condo community?" The man replied that he did, so then the doctor gave him this advice: "Join the board of the Homeowners' Association - believe me, it will be the longest year of your life." I might add that he forgot to tell his patient that he would be glad to go at the end of the year, as well. BLOCK.

Maybe I'll do a Let It Out Column. I know; I'll call it: Fine Whines. I would never bank at an institution that calls itself The Fifth Third Bank. That's too much like the Fourth First Baptist Church. I hate salesclerks or waiters who say, no matter what you ask them, "No problem." Or a telemarketer who calls and swears she isn't selling anything. I try not to listen that far along in the conversation. BLOCK.

I wrote a memoir on Windows once; what about: Corners. I like corners, more so that the middle of the block. There was a place called Five Points in Jacksonville, Florida, where I grew up…maybe I should call it Intersections - that's more accurate and …BLOCK. Maybe I should write about something more provocative. I know - Chocolate Ants. It was New Year's Eve, and we had been invited to a party by a psychologist at the hospital. He wasn't particularly well-liked by other members of the department, but he was my supervisor, so I thought we should go. When we arrived, a few other members of the psychology department were there, but most were from other disciplines, and then there were quite a few people we hadn't met. Most turned out to be neighbors of the host and hostess. I noticed quite a few people were laughing as they passed around a tin full of what looked like candy, but which I learned was full of chocolate-covered ants. I'd never had any and wasn't game for trying them, either. Other people, though, made a big fuss about eating them and holding them up, supposedly by their legs, and putting them down their throats. One woman said that it reminded her of when she was a small girl and had tried to catch small birds and tear their legs off. When she said that, almost the entire roomful of partygoers stopped and looked at her. She looked quite embarrassed and muttered something about the wisdom of revealing something like that at a party with a bunch of psychologists. Soon people went back to their partying almost as if the entire incident hadn't happened. But we couldn't forget it.

One day years later, we were in Ayres Department Store downtown, waiting for an elevator when one stopped on our floor, opened, and we saw the woman from the party. We stood face-to-face for a brief moment, no one getting off and our not getting on, until the doors closed and we were left there, knowing that we all had a brief moment of recognition. BLOCK.

I know - Coincidence. We had just gotten home one Saturday evening and saw that there was a message on our answering machine. It was from Judie Ney, telling us that she'd like to recommend a movie. In fact, she and Sylvia had just returned from an afternoon showing of *My Life So Far*. Ann and I were just returning from seeing the late matinee of the same movie with the Robinsons and over dinner had talked about coincidences and also about six degrees of separation - the latter term referring to the theory that each of us is related to the other by someone we know, no more removed than six times. BLOCK.

Writing is difficult for a lot of people. We've all heard of writer's block - something that seems to happen occasionally to many good writers, and some of them write about it later. There are all these self-help books on writing, telling you to set aside a certain time each day and then no matter what, write during that time. Anne Lamott has written of her times to write and how she'll end up doing everything else in the world trying to get ready for writing, and then when she's finally done all she can do, she just sits there at the word processor or typewriter or with pen and paper and stares at the paper, often unable to write anything at all, or at least write anything that makes sense. Some say you should just write whatever comes into your mind, not bothering too much with punctuation or good grammar or whether the thoughts come out just right or the words are exactly the ones you want. Just get something down on paper, they all seem to be saying, and then you can go back and re-write and edit. But what if you don't seem to have any ideas - now that's a sad thought if I ever heard one.

There must be an easier way - some gimmicks to help you get started anyway. It's hard to write a memoir because I've forgotten so much. I may have forgotten a lot, but it's stored somewhere in the brain. I like to think that my mind is so full and crowded with facts and information (note, I didn't say wisdom) that I can't always gain immediate access. It's like that small jar of maraschino cherries that you know is in the back of the refrigerator somewhere but you can't find it. I never believed in writer's block - I always thought it was a term like *burn-out* that people used to get out of doing something, a lot like malingering, and I guess since I've written three long pages on it, I still don't believe in it.

Things I Know, or Think I Know, or Thought I Knew, or Who Knows?

A – Age - The older I get, the less I know for sure. Advice - never give advice unless you're asked.

B - Beauty isn't always truth, and truth is not always beauty, regardless of how many famous people have said it is or repeated that phrase.

C – Curious - always be curious; curiosity may have killed the cat, but satisfaction brought it back.

D - Don't have too many "don'ts."

E - Every exit is an entrance to somewhere else.

F – Friends - make and keep friends; they are necessary for happiness in life.

G - Good, as in good judgment comes from experience, while experience often comes from bad judgment.

H - Hell is a state of mind; get rid of hate and hostility if you want to be healthy.

I - Nothing wrong with saying "I"; just don't say it too often.

J – Junk - get rid of it; join in on things in life; don't sit back and be passive.

K – Kisses - you can't get or give too many.

L – Laugh - find things to laugh at, even if it's yourself.

M – Memories - they can last a lifetime and can keep getting better if your life gets better.

N - Don't be afraid to say "No" if it's something you really don't want to do.

O – Open - be open and have an open mind.

P - The purpose of life is to have a life of purpose.

Q – Quest - always quest after something.

R – Read - read everything you can.

S – Shortcuts - there are hardly ever any.

T – Trouble - you can try to avoid it, but it will eventually catch up with you, so learn to cope with it. Remember, if you plant poison ivy, you won't harvest strawberries.

U – Undo - try as you will, you can never undo anything.

V – Voice - you've got a voice; don't be afraid to use it.

W – Work - work at something, even after you've retired. The satisfaction you get from work well done (physical or mental) can hardly be equaled.

X – Xeric - learn a few words that start with X, and it will help you out tremendously in Scrabble.

Y – Youth - remember what it was like to be young, but don't yearn for it.

Z – Zest - a life with a little zest is best.

The Train Made a Stop at My Station But I Didn't Get On

"For of all sad words of tongue or pen, the saddest are these: 'It Might Have Been.'" These words were written by John Greenleaf Whittier in "Maud Miller." One always wonders about missed opportunities. We've all thought what would have happened if... . Many of the people I admire have said in interviews that they have no regrets. I always liked someone who said that and wondered if it would be true about me some day. In one sense, saying you have no regrets seems rather egotistical, maybe even implying that your life was perfect. On the other hand, it could also mean that you would make the same choices again.

I don't believe everything is predetermined, already set out no matter what you do, but I also think one's choices are limited by circumstances and unforeseen factors. When one gets to a certain point in life or to a certain age, one can't help but wonder how things may have been different if a different choice had been made many years in the past. Like the quotation above, it seems sad, at least at first glance. But it could just as easily be reason for celebration, as well.

I sometimes used to wonder, while in college studying hard for an exam, or working on some assignment that was due the next day, that maybe I should just chuck it all and go work for my aunt and uncle at the restaurant where I worked each summer during college. Then I thought about how bored I would probably have been because after working there for the three summer months, I could hardly wait to get back to college.

As I was finishing my psychology internship, in June, 1962, I went for a job interview in a tiny town in the middle of nowhere called Milledgeville. It had the only state mental hospital in Georgia at the time. When I saw the signs on the benches around the grounds that said "White" or "Colored", I began to have doubts about living in the South again. The chief psychologist who interviewed me was named Dr. Robert Wildman - perhaps a sign sent to warn me? He didn't talk nearly as much about my duties as he did the benefits of living there - a house on the grounds for only $100 a month, a maid and gardener for only $25 each, and membership at a reduced rate in the all-white Macon Country Club. He stressed the salary and how cultural weekends were only a short drive away to Atlanta. I really didn't have to think about my decision to go there, although when I got my first check after being promoted to a staff position at Larue Carter Hospital in September of that year and saw that the difference in take-home pay wasn't all that different from an intern's, I did have some second thoughts, but only for a few minutes.

I wonder now if I chose the right career. I think I would have liked to have been a journalist and worked for a newspaper. Or would I? So many thoughts and yearnings are formed with insufficient information. What would have happened if we had bought a different house, lived in a different neighborhood, saved a little more money? The questions may be intriguing, but one can only surmise. I read somewhere the other day that ... "even dreams have expiration dates." Like worry, there's no use to dwell on these things, unless they can somehow influence your behavior now or in the future. Someone once said that it was the things you didn't do that you regretted, but I think that just sounds better somehow, maybe not as guilt-inducing. Who's done the research on things like this? So, the train did stop at my station, and I made the choice not to get on because it was only going to somewhere I'd been before that I didn't want to visit again.

All This and Heaven, Too?

We live in a time of unprecedented prosperity, at least in this country. We have a very high standard of living, the greatest material and technological kinds of things, freedom to travel almost anywhere, opportunities our ancestors wouldn't have dreamed of. We have museums and theaters and more books and movies than we could ever read or see, plus the wealth of information on both television and the Internet.

I think a positive outlook is one of the best things one can develop. It can be helpful in many ways; not distorting the truth, but looking at the glass as half full rather than half empty. I've actually tried putting this kind of thinking in my decision-making, and it is always helpful, as long as one doesn't develop unrealistic expectations, such as viewing the cup as totally full when it is only half full.

Lately, I've been going to the pool on many so-called partly cloudy days, interpreting the weather forecasts as partly sunny, and I am way ahead for the entire summer.

Ann and I recently went to a meeting at the Wellness Center (note the name, not Illness Center) and six people shared their stories with our group. At least four out of the six viewed themselves as survivors, rather than victims, and by outward appearances, they certainly seemed to be doing better than the other two.

It's late on a sunny, end-of-the-summer afternoon, and I'm really not saddened by the approaching season's end, but I'm looking forward to bright, sunny, colorful crisp autumn days, good for walking or driving through the countryside, with stops at out-of-the-way small town stands where you can get fresh persimmon ice-cream, or look through antique shops, or take photographs of all the fall colors and long shadows in the late afternoon.

Sometimes I almost wish I were a believer, so that I could enjoy… "all this, and heaven, too."

On the other hand, we're also a nation on the brink of another major war. There really is, most now say, global warming, certainly a lot of which must be due to automobile emissions. The nightly newscasters tell us how half the world is starving, with unacceptable drinking water. There are AIDS epidemics of major proportions in many of the developing countries.

There is still racial prejudice and injustice, and the world isn't always fair. There's Ann's illness, our son's divorce. Maybe it's a good thing I'm not a believer because then I'd have to title this… "All This, and Hell, Too?"

How I Spent My Summer Vacation
(Or Twenty-five Things You Can Do to Avoid Writing)

It's August 12th, and I'm sitting on the deck, and Ann is sitting across from me, stringing blue beads. For what reason, I have no idea. It doesn't look like a necklace in the making. It's probably for some re-decorating project she's envisioned, so I'm afraid to ask.

A lot has happened this summer, and I should be able to write a bunch of memoirs. I work from a title. I usually decide on a working title for a topic or incident or memory. Of course, I may change the title as the memoir progresses, unlike Ann, who writes a volume and then narrows it down and can't decide on what to call it.

Several times I've gone to the computer to start to write, and nothing has come to mind. Once, I noticed that the computer keys needed cleaning, so I quit, temporarily, and cleaned them. I got ready to write again, and then there was a pause, and the only thing I could think of was - what about cleaning out the desk drawers? After I'd done that, I decided I might as well clean out my socks drawer, than my underwear drawer, than all my drawers, which took quite a little while. When I got back to my desk, I thought I might as well clean off the top of it, then the two In/Out boxes, then my card file, and then update my address book.

Of course, I could take a break from trying to write and lie out on the deck and soak up a little sunshine. Then I could get some lunch, and while I'm eating, I could read the newspaper. Then, there's that *New Yorker* that just came in the mail - maybe I could get some new ideas for stories from it. Also, there are all the other old *New Yorkers* that I need to read and clear out so they won't clutter up the house. Maybe I could read the magazines and books on writing that I bought at the Friends of the Library Book Sale last month - good places to get ideas on writing and also to improve my first sentences, that is, *if I could get that far along.*

Maybe I should check the mail before I actually start writing, and then check the e-mail, too. There may be some Scrabble E-mail games with other players from around the world just waiting on my play to get the game rolling.

There's always the box of bills that needs to be straightened out; then I must remember to get some more postage stamps. Maybe I should send a card to Gonya, who's missed the last few Scrabble Club meetings. I heard she had been ill.

Well, all those things are done. What shall I write about? I should try to write something funny. Or maybe I could write something serious; after all, I did read two interesting books this summer. One was by George Sheehan, the cardiologist turned runner and fitness expert who's just learned he has inoperable cancer and is tying to decide how to live his life for what time he has left. He's always been a person who values his privacy and time spent alone, either running or writing. Should he change now, he thinks, and pursue more noble things? Can he change even if he wanted to? He ponders all the big questions about why are we on the earth, what is the reason for our being, and what is life all about. Is it too late? Would people, even those closest to him, welcome the changes, even if he could make them? As he writes in *Going the Distance,* the concern over his impending death, no matter how far in the future or uncertain, generates meditation on the great questions of life. Should one continue to do what one does best? Should there be no regrets?

He said that the important thing was not so much to be good as it was to be happy. That sounds like a philosophy I'd like. It's certainly a provocative statement, especially when taken out of context. The main assertion for his argument is that you can be good without doing anything (for example, by not stealing or not lying) whereas to be happy you first have to *do* something. Happiness, he says, is the by-product of some action.

I read another book by an astrophysicist who said he could explain the universe in just six numbers. The book was supposedly written for the laymen - in everyday language that the average person could understand. I'd say it was at the level the average astrophysicist might read and earn credit at the same time for continuing education. I could only read about ten to twelve pages at a time, so that the little book of only one hundred and sixty-five pages took quite a while to finish and absorb.

The thesis of the book was fascinating because it espoused not just a theory but marshaled all kinds of interesting facts to state that the value of just six numbers all had to be between extremely narrow limits for human beings to evolve and thrive. Not only that, but the book stated that there are probably multiverses, not just other universes, out there. A lot of what exists now and what we are experiencing now, for example, was because, the author says, of events that happened 10 to the 24th power of the first second after the Big Bang, if you can even fathom that idea.

Whew! Pondering all these difficult questions is very tiring. I'd better stop and take a rest, before I notice anything else that needs to be cleaned or straightened or sorted or answered.

Hell Is Just a State of Mind

When you're around twelve years of age in the Episcopal religion, you go through a series of lectures and discussions with mostly other twelve-year-olds, as well as a few older teenagers and adults. They are called confirmation classes. A lot of what was being said was somewhat boring because I had heard it all before, not having missed a single day of Sunday School for several years. But what had just been said was something new, something unexpected. Mr. Corbin, Director of Religious Education, said that hell was "…really just a state of mind." I'd suspected that both heaven and hell were not the concrete opposites I'd been told about or heard about from my friends who were Baptist, Methodist, Presbyterian, or Roman Catholic. My Jewish friends never discussed religion with me. I always thought about heaven, hell, purgatory, and all those other religious terms from then on as metaphors or not really real. I listened more intently to the sermons from then on, but unlike the talk about hell, they were given by the senior minister, who name strangely was Dr. Valentine Lee, or by the new assistant minister, Mr. Taylor, who had only recently come over from England. Both of them talked mostly about money and how much more wonderful it was to give than to receive and how the money in the other half of our pledge envelopes went to missionary work in Africa, mainly.

I never got much else out of the sermons or Sunday School lessons until I was in college, and the minister at the small Episcopal chapel told us that the next Sunday's sermon was going to be on the unforgivable sin, and that we should do a little research during the week to see what we could come up with that would constitute the unforgivable sin. I started out very concretely and looked in the biggest bible I could find in the library and asked a lot of my more religious friends of other denominations what the unforgivable sin was. Most came up with hunches; in fact, all came up with different answers, some even with biblical quotes, but when I looked, I couldn't find any sin labeled strictly that way, with those exact words. I was all ears at the next Sunday's sermon, where the minister never really gave an answer until about nine tenths of the way through, when he said that the unforgivable sin was the sin of which you are unable to forgive yourself. I understood what he was saying, and I thought he was quite clever, but I also thought that it was really more a matter of semantics or some intellectual word game than religion or belief, and this made me question all religious ideas even more. Many years later, I came to understand this concept much better, in my work as a clinical psychologist, but that was still a long way off.

When it came time to choose electives the next semester, I chose a course on comparative religion. It was an introductory course, and the students in it came from every major, only a few seeming to have a genuine interest in anything religious. The professor was also the minister of a small church in Gainesville, Florida. In his class, I learned that Matthew, Mark, Luke, and John didn't agree on a lot. In fact, I learned that you could find a basis for almost any idea at all, even conflicting ideas, in the Bible. I thought or was told or overheard or somehow came to the notion that the Bible wasn't to be taken literally. It had a lot of good ideas in it, but is also had some bad ideas in it.

A few years later, at Vanderbilt as a graduate student, I took an anthropology course on magic and religion. We discussed some ideas, such as an eye for an eye and a tooth for a tooth. It seems that these were rather progressive ideas at the time they were first mentioned, as up until that time, if one clan member was hurt, and, say, lost an eye in some dispute, then the clan would go out and kill someone, or maybe two or three, in the other clan, so that an eye for an eye was not as harsh and was actually seen as fairer than revenge on a larger scale. We also studied people in countries like Brazil, where the majority of inhabitants were so poor here on earth and had so little hope of even changing that, that the only thing worth spending a lot of time on was on things associated with the afterlife, since it would only be in heaven that they could ever get a decent break. Somewhere along the way in studying these things, I went from a practicing Episcopalian to an atheist, with hardly any time between them at all. I always thought, and still do, that an agnostic is just a cowardly atheist, or a cowardly Christian, depending on your point of view.

Browsing at Barnes and Noble

I love books and magazines, too. One of the fun things I like to do is to ask a couple of friends to go with Ann and me to a restaurant and then instead of having after-dinner coffee and dessert, go instead to the Barnes and Noble Bookstore. Then we tell everyone to go through all the books or magazines they want and to meet in the café, where we all spread out our choices and have an iced mocha frappe or a cappuccino. Desserts are delicious there, too, but if you've just come from a big meal, the coffee may be enough. It's always interesting to see what has interested other people as well and discuss why they chose those books to look at further.

Of course, the best thing is you don't have to buy the books; you can just browse through them. Usually what I do is to get on the Internet when I get home and see if the books I want are in the library, or if they're new, if they're on order. I can find out where all twenty-five copies of a book are and then call the library and have them hold one for me, but it's even better to call with several selections and get them all delivered to one of the branches close to where we live. If you want a bestseller or an Oprah's Club book, you might be told you're number forty on the list, but sometimes they buy thirty copies of the same book, so you really never have to wait very long. The longest I've ever waited was about four weeks and that was for *Midnight in the Garden of Good and Evil,* but that was on the bestseller list for almost two years.

I kept a list of the books I read for one entire year - about fifty. I tried to keep the list as diverse as possible, in case I died in the process and someone looked over the list - I wanted them to think of me as someone with a wide range of interests. After all, you can tell a lot about a person by what he/she reads, but you'd need a good-sized sample to make any valid interpretations. What on earth would people think if they saw a list of the books I read just last December? Well, here it is: *Angela's Ashes,* by Frank McCourt, *A Brief History of Time,* by Stephen Hawking, *Brain Droppings,* by George Carlin, and *Make the Connection,* by Bob Greene and Oprah Winfrey - probably the only month of the year that I didn't read any fiction.

Dust

I read somewhere the other day that the average child at birth weighs 7.4 pounds and that the cremated remains of a person weigh 7.4 pounds. The irony of those two statements in juxtaposition reminded me of the biblical saying, "Dust thou art and to dust thou shalt return." It also reminded me of the joke about the little boy who, upon hearing this for the first time, yelled to his mother from the bedroom, saying, "You'd better come quick - there are a lot of people under my bed, but I can't tell if they're coming or going."

Anyway, it's enough to make you wonder if anything important or significant happened between birth, the beginning of life, and death, the end of life. A lot of pounds, I can tell you that. I thought I'd see what I could remember from my childhood. I remember when I first started school, I lived on King Street in Jacksonville, Florida. The street was not named after Martin Luther. Jacksonville is located just thirty-five miles from Georgia and 350 miles from Miami, so it wasn't full of tourists but was more like many small towns in the south back in the early 1940's.

Most children had not attended kindergarten when they started first grade in the public grammar school, unless they had attended a parochial kindergarten. Looking back, my first grade class of about thirty students seemed quite diverse. There were children of many different religions—Episcopal, Roman Catholic, Lutheran, Presbyterian, Southern Baptist, Methodist, Mormon, and quite a few Jewish children. There were children from a wide range of socioeconomic levels and from many different nationalities. Some of the last names I remember are Bailey, Jensen, Kartsonis, Krantz, Pollock, and Rotstein. Some of the first names were Renee, Elvira, Claudette, Verlin, Carol Ann, Myron, and Dalton. Most of the children walked the few blocks to school, although a few were dropped off by their parents who drove cars with the top half of the headlights painted black because of the Second World War. In fact, air raid drills were practiced at school, and all the children were herded into the inner hallways where the floors were of highly polished wood. We had to practice sitting down on the floor with our knees pulled up to our chests and our heads down on the top of our knees. Of course, with all the small children crowded together and in the dark, as the lights were turned off and thick black oil cloth shades covered the big windows, there was a lot of moving and shuffling around. One day I got a huge splinter in my rear end doing this. Of course, I was too embarrassed to ask one of the teachers (who were all women) to help me, so I suffered all the rest of the day until I got home in the afternoon.

In our neighborhood there was a family whose last name was Sigmundjack. They had two boys very close in age, but because of their German-sounding name and the accent their parents had, I was discouraged from playing with them. Everyone seemed very concerned about the war, and we had a big victory garden in the vacant lot next to our house. My father was in the Merchant Marine and during wartime he wore a uniform. His freighter stopped carrying domestic goods and began carrying items to do with the war effort, such as C-rations. We'd receive letters from him with some of the sentences or words blacked out by some precursor to the black magic marker.

My mother, who always seemed pretty honest to us, always fudged on the shoe coupons we were issued. Sometimes when my father's ship came in to New York or Boston or Baltimore, we'd go visit him, and some of the ship's crew would give us some of their unused coupons, not in the coupon books with our names on them, of course. She would pretend to tear them out of our book, and when the shoe salesman would protest, she would counter with, " Well, that's the way we do it in the South," saying this with a somewhat exaggerated Southern accent. I distinctly remember being worried one time when getting a new pair of shoes, and was relieved to hear the salesman say that he couldn't have taken the coupons if he hadn't actually seen my mother tear them out herself.

It's strange the little things and details that one remembers. Since I went all through grammar school, junior high, and high school with most of my first grade class, and even though the high school graduating class had over 400 students, I wonder how many I'll remember when I go to my 50th high school reunion next August (2003). Maybe many will already have returned to dust.

Are You Allergic to Mouse Protein?

Just before starting on the new kind of treatment that we had all agreed held some promise for getting rid of Ann's lymphoma, she was given a questionnaire to complete. The first in a series of questions was: "Are you allergic to mouse protein?" Now how in the hell would you know if you're allergic to mouse protein unless (1) you had previously eaten a mouse or (2) you had been treated with Rituxan before. And, if you had been treated with Rituxan before, they wouldn't have asked you this question, because the questionnaire clearly stated… "For First Time Rituxan Users."

We had gotten up early that morning because Ann had an 8:15 AM. appointment with her oncologist, Dr. Lee. We were sure he was going to recommend another course of chemotherapy, or radiation, or maybe even a bone marrow transplant, so we were prepared to spend most of the day, if not the entire day, at his office and clinic, just across the street from St. Vincent Hospital.

Not long before, I had searched on the Internet for new treatments for non-Hodgkin's lymphoma, because we had just learned that the chemotherapy hadn't put Ann into remission as we thought it would. I found two new medications, one just recently approved by the FDA, and the other in its last round of clinical trials. We had heard about the latter on the TV program "Sixty Minutes" just a few weeks earlier. However, this particular morning we learned that the trial drug was not available unless we wanted to travel to Michigan, change physicians, etc. On the other hand, Dr. Lee had just recently attended a workshop on Rituxan and had even had a few patients on it. So, we all agreed that Rituxan, this new monoclonal antibody therapy, was worth a try. The way this new drug worked was: they injected lymphoma cells into mice; then the mice's immune systems developed antibodies to the lymphoma cells. A protein was taken from these antibodies, cloned, and then injected into the patient. It was supposed to jump start the patient's own immune system to start producing its own antibodies. At least this is the simplified version that I was able to read about on the Internet.

After she had her exam, we talked with Dr. Lee, then were ushered over to the other side, which is the chemotherapy clinic, with a separate waiting room and separate staff, except for the doctors. I had brought a book and Ann had got ready to select a recliner to sit in when the nurse said that the first treatment required Ann to go to St. Vincent's to get the drug because of the dangers of an allergic reaction. She would be right there in the hospital and could get immediate attention, if needed. So, we gathered our things and drove the short distance over to the Outpatient Oncology Department where Ann was handed the questionnaire to fill out - the questionnaire with the strange question about mouse protein.

Memories of Childhood

My family, which consisted of my twin sisters, four years younger, my mother, my maternal grandmother, and my father (who was away most of the time in the Merchant Marine) rented houses until we were finally able to buy a big two-story house in a section of Jacksonville called Riverside, just before I started fourth grade.

I have only a few memories about the house we lived in when I was four. It was on Barr St. and the day we moved in, a neighbor brought over a big pot of vegetable soup. I remember being photographed on a pony by a traveling photographer, cowboy hat included. I recall stepping on a bee that left its stinger in my foot when I was playing barefoot outside; but most of all I remember becoming friends with a couple named Hildebrandt. In fact, I met Mrs. Hildebrandt on the first day I moved in because I wrote something in chalk on the fence that separated our backyard from the alley behind the house. The woman, who had a very strong German accent, not knowing we had just moved there, told me to go home and leave that property alone. I defiantly told her that I could do whatever I wanted because I lived there. I can't remember what happened then except that she became a friend where I could go and get freshly baked cookies and talk to her and her husband. My mother and grandmother were neighborly but somewhat distant because, after all, we were just about to enter World War II, and Germans were the enemy.

We didn't live there long before we moved to another house farther out but still in the city, two blocks from where I was to start first grade. After we moved into this stucco house on Wolfe St., my mother found out that in actuality I'd have to attend a school too far away to walk and would have to ride a city bus or be driven there. Since we didn't own a car then, and since I wouldn't reach my sixth birthday until December, she decided I wouldn't go to school until the next September. We then moved to a house on King Street. on a corner with a large vacant lot next door. It had a big screened front porch, and I remember spending many days and evenings in a swing or a rocking chair on that porch.

I was then able to walk to Central Riverside Elementary School. When I finally got to first grade, I loved every minute of it, unlike some of the children who cried on the first day of school or for most of that first week. I had escaped from my twin sisters, mother, and grandmother and took to school like a fish to water.

We had a Victory Garden in the vacant lot next door, where we grew tomatoes, radishes, small green onions, beets, carrots, corn, mustard greens, collard greens, and what we called snap beans—called green beans elsewhere. We had such an abundance of fresh vegetables that I made spending money by selling them around the neighborhood, carrying an assortment of them in my red wagon with the varnished wooden slats on the sides.

In the summer between the third and fourth grades, the rent for the three bedroom bungalow went up from $35 to $37.50 a month, so my parents decided it was time to move—to buy our first house at 2217 Dellwood Ave., about nine blocks away, but still in the same school district. I had a big sleeping porch with eight windows for my bedroom; we painted it blue, and I put on the walls all my pennants my father had bought me from ports in his travels in the Merchant Marine.

I attended the Church of the Good Shepherd, an Episcopal church, from first through 12th grade. It was a big gothic church with leaded glass windows and was made out of yellow, sand-colored stone. The earlier brick church on the corner of the next street was attached by a connecting building with three stories, which became the Sunday School. The best thing about the addition was that it had a huge indoor swimming pool, thanks to a wealthy donor who left an endowment for its care and upkeep. I took swimming lessons there, and our Boy Scout troop was the only one in town where we could go swimming after our weekly meetings.

I became an acolyte (or altar boy) and didn't miss a single Sunday of Sunday School for the three high school years. We were the only Episcopalians in my grammar school grades - the others were Baptists (two or more varieties), Roman Catholics, Lutherans, Methodists, Presbyterians, or from Latter Day Saints, Church of God or Christain churches, or from Jewish synagogues. It didn't take me long to think of our church as a lot more liberal than the others, many of which taught that dancing or drinking wasn't acceptable. The restrictions didn't seem to phase my classmates or their parents, though. I soon learned what the word hypocrisy meant.

Everyone at our church dressed up on Sundays - the men and boys wearing suits and ties and all the women wearing hats. Girls over twelve had to wear a hat or scarf at all times inside the church. Our church was not air-conditioned, so ordinary hand-held fans, as well as some very ornate fans, were used mainly by the women.

We had real wine, not grape juice, for communion. I never really understood the Trinity - the three in one - or even the Holy Ghost, and I did ask some questions, but they were overshadowed by the beautiful music and candles and pomp and circumstance and the trumpet procession on Easter morning, so I just mouthed the words and sang all the hymns and didn't question the doctrine.

Episcopalian traditions seemed much more intellectual and less emotional - we were christened, sprinkled, really, when just a baby, not baptized or immersed in water; we weren't "saved" at big tent revivals. We took classes and were "confirmed" at age twelve - confirming on our own behalf what our parents had done for us at christening.

But all these religious beliefs were about to change when I got to college and took a couple of comparative religion courses and met people from more diverse backgrounds.

Metaphor and the Real Thing

February in Indiana is drab, overcast, and rainy, and sometimes there are even ice storms. Ice storms are both beautiful - the way the ice glistens on the bare tree limbs - and scary, as when it builds up too much and causes the limbs to break, making a sound like a shot of gun fire. A really bad ice storm can sound like a battlefield, especially at night when the noise of the day has died down and there are sometimes echoes.

February 13th was our son's 39th birthday. He was at work and in the process of counting the day's proceeds when the last waiter came in and gave him his receipts. One of the owners happened to be there, too, planning the next day, which was Valentine's Day and what was expected to be a big day, customer-wise, and was discussing with others what the special would be. Charley had gone into the back office and said he would finish up the books. As he looked up from the desk, he heard the back door open. There appeared a guy, at least a foot shorter than Charley and with pantyhose pulled down over his face, who asked Charley where the safe was. Charley's immediate response was that this was a joke being played on him, so he tried to peer up under the pantyhose at the guy's face, to see if he could tell who it might be. At that point the guy acted irritated and seemed to think Charley was crazy and pulled out a silver revolver and held it up to the side of Charley's head. It was then that Charley knew this was no birthday prank, but a real robbery.

When the guy repeated his question about where the safe was, Charley told him there was no safe. The guy then asked where the cash register was, and Charley told him all the money was in the cash box on the desk. By this time, Charley had been ordered to lie on the floor, but he raised himself up and gave the guy the key to the box and told him to take it all - to take anything he wanted. He yelled at Charley to lie flat on the floor, which was impossible, because Charley was too tall and the office too small to accommodate his full length. The robber took the money and since it was not the day's receipts, but the cash box full of ones and fives that they kept to make change on busy nights, it looked like a lot more money than it actually was. The gunman then fled out the back door. He had already scared off one of the kitchen staff as he had entered. As Rosario had gone to empty some trash, the robber asked him where the manager was, and Rosario had pushed him aside and then run around the building and into the Time Out Lounge to call 911. All of these events took only a few minutes. There happened to be an off-duty policeman in the lounge next door who got all the numbers of the license plate, but not the one letter. He even fired a shot at the fleeing car while noting its color as it sped off.

Just as Charley thought it safe to get up off the floor and grabbed the telephone to dial 911, the owner came back to the office, noticed how strange Charley looked, and asked what was wrong. As Charley blurted out what was happening, she ran over and asked him how to push the silent alarm button, which Charley had never even had time to think of.

As Ann and I were sitting in Charley and Jenny's living room the next afternoon, babysitting for Savannah while Charley headed back to work at the restaurant and Jenny went off to teach her class at the Art Center, we thought of the shots that rang out on a cold February night long ago and were thankful none had rung out last night at the restaurant.

What's the Prognosis?

Ann's been in the hospital three times since February, and it's been hard on her. Nausea, vomiting, chills, fevers, headaches, hives, and not being able to eat have taken their toll, but she's better now and on a new treatment regimen. The prognosis is good.

I, however, have been left alone - in the kitchen, especially. I've been frustrated, disappointed, unhappy, depressed, anxious, and have feelings of very low self-esteem. I never knew that just two extra minutes in the microwave could ruin an entire dinner or dry out a casserole beyond belief.

I knew the dryer was vented to the outside, but who knew there was a lint tray that had to be pulled out and cleaned after almost every load? I did wonder why the towels were taking longer and longer to dry, but I thought it was just my imagination.

I took over the vacuuming a long time ago and could zip around the house pretty fast. Why was the vacuum cleaner not picking up strings and things off the carpet? No matter how hard I pressed down or how many times I went over the same place, it didn't work right. Who knew it would sound like it was working even if it had a broken belt? No lights came on to tell you that, as they do on a computer.

You can vacuum, clean, dust, wash, and scrub - and just a few days later, you've got to do it all over again. I did learn my least favorite job, though - cleaning the litter box when you have two eighteen-pound cats. Changing the filter in the furnace is the easiest job in the world compared to all the usual household chores.

I've started reading *Hints from Heloise* because I want maintenance to be as efficient as possible. I now spray lemon *Pledge* on all the bathroom mirrors and the glass enclosing the shower because it makes it 100 per cent easier to clean the next time. Using *Simonize* works on the bathtub to give it the best shine ever. You have to take precautions, though, and not spray the floor of the tub, and then fill it once with water before you use it for a bath, and it won't be slippery.

If you've got guests coming or if you need a little break from cleaning, you can hire people for just a small fortune who'll clean for you. It helps if one of them speaks English a little.

Medical science and medications seem to be working for Ann. I just wish they'd invent a solution for retarded husbands. The prognosis is poor.

It Is Now, But It Wasn't
Then (Funny, That Is)

"I want my money back. There's no way in the world I'd ever wear that suit again." The clerk reminded me that it was brand new. "No way would I ever feel comfortable in it." The clerk then changed his stance and asked if I would be interested in another suit. "No, I do *not* want another suit."

It started when I was sitting in a Howard Johnson's in Kokomo in about 1967, eating a piece of banana creme pie and having a cup of coffee on my way to what was then called Bunker Hill Air Force Base. All of a sudden the nylon zipper to my new blue suit just popped open. Luckily, I was sitting at the counter and it was before the late afternoon rush. I had to ask three waitresses before I found one with a safety pin, which I immediately took to the men's room and tried to use to pin the fly closed. The lightweight nylon zipper appeared to be flimsy, and there was no way I could force it back into working. By this time, it was getting late, so I rushed off to teach my first class in abnormal psychology at the Kokomo I. U. Extension, which just happened to meet that semester at Bunker Hill.

When I got to the main gate, almost on time, they couldn't find any clearance for me to continue. After several phone calls and another wait, I was finally let through and given directions to the classroom. When I arrived, there was a sergeant in front of the class. He was standing on raised flooring, with a blackboard behind him, but no lectern or anything else. He motioned for me to come in, and I motioned for him to come out. Now, evidently Air Force Sergeants like to have the upper hand, but when he saw that I definitely wasn't coming in, he came to the doorway of the classroom.

I explained what had happened and told him if he could just arrange for a desk to be put up on the platform, I was sure I could teach the three-hour class. The class was becoming fidgety and restless, but just a few minutes later, two other uniformed men moved a desk in, and I, with briefcase strategically placed in front of me, entered and started the class. I wasn't being paranoid as I noticed all the students were staring at me.

I always told the students, who were a mixture of air force personnel, their relatives, and a few regular students from Kokomo, that they would have to participate in classroom discussions and that I would call on them from time to time, and that the correctness of their comments in the discussions was secondary; it was their participation that could earn them as much as 10 per cent of their grade, and thus it could make the difference between an A and a B or a D and an F. This always calls forth discussion on its own, so things went pretty much as usual for the first half of the class.

When the time came for a break, I thought, what the hell, maybe I should just explain what had happened, and I did just that. There was laughter, and when they saw I wasn't going to attempt to get up and leave the room, three or four of them offered to get me a Coke or something from the vending machines. It turned out to be one of the best classes I ever taught, partly because most of those taking it really were interested in the subject matter, but also I think because we got off to a candid start.

Needless to say, the clerk refunded my money, even if the trousers had already been cuffed to fit me. It's funny now, but it wasn't then.

My Last Memoir

Losing Ann is the saddest thing that's ever happened to me. Watching her die caused a part of me to die, too. One can never be fully prepared for the death of a loved one, even if you've been expecting it. It was a shock. The only thing that kept me functioning in the first few hours and days after her death is that a certain numbness, of which you are not fully aware at the time, comes over you and shields you from the final realization.

It's been fifteen months since Ann died. At the hospice, after having been brought in on the afternoon of February 25th, Ann's respirations were so fast and labored that I didn't see how she could possibly continue breathing that way. In the early morning of the 26th, the nurse told me that even though Ann couldn't respond, that the last sense to go was the auditory sense, so that perhaps she could hear me if I wanted to tell her anything. When the nurse left the room a little later, I went over and stood over the bed where she lay propped up and whispered to her very quietly. The last thing I told her was that she could go now - she didn't need to stay around for us. The minute I finished saying this, she took one huge breath, opened her eyes and let the breath out slowly, breathed in one more time, then relaxed and stopped breathing. All the red blotches on her face disappeared, and most of the wrinkles in her face, and the crease between her eyes went away, and she looked peaceful at last.

I stood there a few minutes, trying to regain what little composure I could and then went to the nursing station to summon the nurse. She came into the room and looked at Ann, took her arm, felt the pulse in her neck, closed Ann's eyes, and said, "It's over - she's gone."

After they prepared Ann to be seen by the medical director - she would be taken to the medical center for research and teaching purposes - I came home. There were people to be called - a son, a sister, a best friend, and other relatives and friends. I had to e-mail our daughter, who was at sea, working on a cruise ship. I wondered how do I tell the cats who meet me at the door when I return? They can sense something is not right.

A memorial service or funeral helps some to have closure, I would imagine, but Ann specifically did not want these. A well-written letter arrives from a physician at the medical center, saying what a great service your loved one is providing and offering condolences. It didn't seem like a form letter, either. Telephone calls and cards start arriving. Many cards are very beautiful with thoughtful verses in them, but it is the handwritten notes of a more personal nature that are so appreciated and treasured that you keep and read over and over, trying to glean some satisfaction from them.

At some point I rest, but sleep comes only in fits and starts. Eventually, I have to get up - there are things to do, cats to feed, calls to return, an obituary to write, plans to be made. But most of all, there is all this quiet and time and aloneness. I start to miss Ann when I want to share a thought or ask an opinion about something not really that important.

I go about some sort of daily routine. I tell myself I won't have any "what ifs" - but they come anyway, much later on when I least expect them. It's the same with tears - I try not to break down. Thoughts come tumbling in at odd times and when I don't want them to - like pain in a phantom limb. What I want has been amputated, and I'll never, ever be whole again. Perhaps I'll be able to compensate for my *disability*, and others may not always see it or don't recognize it. It's like when I used to see someone pull into a handicapped parking space and then run into the building and I think that he's not really handicapped. But I become more tolerant because I know that one can't always see another's pain and hurt. I try to put up a good front until all the effort is just too much. I'll never be the same because part of me is gone - it's been amputated. If I'm lucky, I'll find an artificial limb or get really good at using crutches. I can compensate and go on, but I'll have to do everything with something missing - I'll always be an amputee.

One of Ann's favorite authors, Anne Lamott, just published a new book, *Plan B*, in which she sums it up better than anyone I've read. She writes, "If you haven't already, you will lose someone you can't live without, and your heart will be badly broken, and you never completely get over the loss of a deeply beloved person. But this is also good news. The person lives forever, in your broken heart that didn't seal back up. And you come through, and you learn to dance with the banged up heart. You dance to the absurdities of life; you dance to the minuet of old friendships."

Grow, Damn It!

I don't believe in an afterlife - not for the body or the soul, mainly because I don't think we have a soul that survives any more than a body that survives. Just as the mind is a function of the brain, the soul (or spirit or whatever you want to call it) is a function of the body, and when the body goes, there goes the soul. I'd like to believe that one lives on in the minds of those left behind, whether it's something the deceased has said or done or created or in some way influenced the person remembering. One also lives on in what he or she leaves behind, including all the things and objects that person has collected, not just money or land or a house. Memories, though, eventually fade away, much faster than any of us would like to believe. Famous people probably take longer to recede in memory, and those who leave behind some record - a movie, a song, an invention - may live on longer. If you created something like the zipper or the safety pin or refrigerator, you might live on slightly longer than someone who only created a recipe for hush puppies, but maybe not even then. Who can name the inventor of the zipper or safety pin?

A few weeks after Ann died, our daughter Elizabeth and I were sitting around going over the cards and notes people had written us about Ann and looking over the list of people who had called to offer their condolences, and Elizabeth remarked that it was strange that Jean Baxter hadn't written or called, and I agreed. I told Liz that Jean had taken her maiden name back when she had been divorced and that her last name was now Morningstar. Jean had been a nurse's aide who worked with Ann when they were both at Regency Place when it was a brand new nursing home in Castleton. They became rather unlikely friends because Mary appeared at first glance to be the quintessential *valley girl* - young, quite attractive, with long blond hair. Upon first meeting her, most people would probably stereotype her as being rather superficial, but Ann said she was a very good nurse - caring and competent and concerned about the patients.

I can't remember who left first - Ann, who moved on to part-time work elsewhere, or Jean , whose husband finished his residency in orthopedics and joined a private practice group. They decided to build a home near Geist, and they even bought a smaller home a few blocks away from where they were building to be near the site and keep an eye on the construction. Ann would occasionally get calls telling her about all the troubles they were having with the builder and things not being done to their specifications. I only half-way kiddingly said that they would be the home-buyers from hell.

Throughout the years Jean would drop in from time to time and tell Ann about the landscaping of the new home and how she was going to North Carolina to buy furniture or somewhere else to buy Oriental carpets. Ann finally had a tour of their new home one day - a huge home perched on a slight hill with only eight other homes around it, accessed by driving over a small bridge. It had a home theater, a library, a huge area that served as a workshop for her husband, and a mud room and a shower downstairs just for the use of their Labrador retriever.

The years seemed to pass quickly. Her husband was doing extremely well in his practice. They didn't have children and a lot of things happened that ended with their getting a divorce and her getting a pretty big settlement - so much so that she said she really didn't have to work anymore unless she wanted to. She began a business where she planted flowers - pots, planters, window boxes, whatever, and then took care of them for a fee. It did quite well, so she began working part-time for a nursery, helping other well-to-do customers design patios and gardens for their homes. Once, when Ann was undergoing a rather rigorous treatment and spending four to five hours a day getting chemo and IV's, we came home to find all our outside pots and window boxes filled with twice the number of plants we would have put into them. She finally accepted payment only for the wholesale price of the plants. The plants were especially beautiful that year and lasted right up until the first hard freeze, blooming over and over.

I looked through Ann's address book and realized that the last we had heard, Jean had bought an older home in an established neighborhood and while there was an address, there was no telephone number. Then I noticed that Ann had a cell phone number for her. I called the number, got voice mail, and left a message about Ann. Later, Jean told us she had been working with a nursery customer who was buying some very large rocks for a rock garden and some had sayings on them - brief poetic sayings, but one rock just said, "Grow, Damn it." The rather arrogant customer asked Jean why they would sell a rock with something so common and vulgar, and the owner, who was within earshot, said, "That happens to be our best seller." Then Jean chimed in, saying that she had a friend who would love that rock. Jean thought to herself that she would have to get one for Ann. The customer said she couldn't imagine Jean's knowing anyone like that. Just then Jean's cell phone rang, and she noted the number. She finished with the customer before listening to the message, thinking what a coincidence. When she got through writing up the sale, she went to her office where she listened, stunned, to the message. She called later that evening to say that Ann had visited her that day.

It makes an interesting story, but I could just as well have written about the beautiful monarch butterfly that landed on my arm the other day while I was on the deck or the Canada goose that honked at me as I looked skyward to see a gaggle flying by. I know it was just a coincidence. There is no way on earth that Ann's spirit would visit Jean Morningstar before she visited me.

She Knew What She Wanted

"But I don't want to paint a barn. I've brought some pictures and photographs of things I'd like to try my hand at," Ann said. I had given Ann a watercolor course being held at a local art supplies store, and the name of the artist teaching the course is one you would probably recognize, as she is well-known locally. The woman had put a slide of a barn on the screen in the front of the room and had said in a very authoritative voice, "We're going to learn to paint a barn today." She went through a series of other pictures - a bowl of pears and apples, a landscape, etc. and said, "These are the things we'll be painting over the next few weeks." When Ann expressed disappointment and asked if the instructor could make an exception, the artist said, "No, this is what we'll do." Ann said jokingly that she wouldn't hold the instructor responsible for the paintings. After no response, Ann began gathering her things together, and the woman asked what she was doing. Ann said that she was leaving. The woman told her she couldn't leave. Ann said, "Just watch me." The woman then said, "You had a gift certificate, and that money is not refundable. You have to take this class first before you take any of my other classes." Ann said, "I won't be taking any of your other classes," and then told her if she needed the money that badly, that she could keep it.

This all happened in the early 1980's. Ann had always wanted to learn to watercolor, and I had given her the certificate for some special occasion, perhaps a birthday. She didn't really try her hand at it again until about 2001, when a neighbor said she had a friend who needed to teach several students how to paint in order to satisfy some course requirement or certification, so the neighbor said she was organizing women from our condo community to form a group that met every Friday morning in the clubhouse. None of the women had taken any painting instruction previously. This time Ann specifically asked if she could paint anything she wanted, and the neighbor said she didn't see why not, since they were just forming the group, and the instructor had a very flexible attitude. So, Ann started going to the group, which mainly consisted of the instructor's placing an object or array of objects in the center of a group of tables, with the eight or so budding artists sitting around in a square. Ann started on her own thing, but listened carefully, as the instructor had chosen the objects so that she could teach them several techniques. Ann had already been helped a little by her sister, in terms of knowing how to mix paints and to *erase* or modify something that you didn't want in the painting. She learned how to do effects with a sponge and how to splatter paint from a brittle brush and how to sprinkle salt - for what effect exactly I don't know.

Ann took in a photograph of a nun that looked difficult to paint and a page ripped from an *Architectural Digest.* When the other students saw the page with an old building and fountain with a nude sculpture in the middle, several remarked that those looked awfully difficult to paint, and they were glad to be painting some of the simpler things on the table. The photograph contained a nun walking across a marble piazza with all the lines and veins of minerals running through it. The other women said that the floor alone looked far too difficult, but Ann persevered. She decided to substitute another nun for the nude sculpture and fountain. She may have thought that would be easier to paint, but both the paintings show a female figure leaving the picture. Having once been a psychologist, I wondered if I was reading too much into it, perhaps.

I remember her bringing the paintings home partially done and then seeing the first one complete after about two or three sessions. The paper was quite wrinkled, and they didn't show up very well, but I noted the great detail and marveled at the job she had done.

Ann was undergoing chemotherapy at the time and then a series of radiation treatments, so she missed some of the art sessions, but new members kept coming in and some of the original members dropped out, saying they didn't think they had any talent in this particular medium. Ann then started on six months of thalidomide, an experimental treatment, and this caused her to have peripheral neuritis, resulting in no feeling in the tips of her fingers (and toes, too, for that matter.) She also had a mild hand tremor - the side effect of some of the six other medications she was taking at the time.

After Ann died, I was going through her study and found a big folder with all the watercolors she had done, a few I had not even seen. There were only about twenty, and their sizes ranged from about the size of a Christmas card to about a twelve by sixteen inch painting. I took two of them to be matted and framed at The Great Frame-Up do-it-yourself store, and with a little help from one of the employees there, chose mats and frames and left the paintings to be flattened out for about twenty-four hours. I thought the two paintings looked good hanging together, so I hung them in a corner of our great room.

I wonder what Ann could have accomplished if she had had just a little more instruction, perhaps a little more patience, and a little more time.

What Fresh Hell Is This?

Ann's Last Thoughts As Written by Art and How He'd Imagine Her
Thoughts -After Having Read All Her Journals

I know it's time to go, but I wanted just one more remission. But, it's time to go. I wish I had a little longer - it's only been three weeks since Dr. Lee said I had about two more months to live. Damn.   I'm confused; I can't think straight. Maybe there is something like a soul that survives.   Yeah, right!

Poor Art - I wish he'd come with me, but I know he wants to live a few more years, and he deserves to. I wish he'd stop pushing fluids and food.   For the past two or three days I've felt as though life was draining out of me.   At times, I'm almost afraid to lie down for fear I'll never get up again. I thought when I went off the thalidomide, I'd have more energy and not be as weak, but I'm weaker than ever and shaky and have trouble focusing my eyes, and nothing has any taste.   What fresh hell is this?

I can't believe it just ends like this.   It's like Gertrude Stein answered when Alice B. Toklas kept asking, as Gertrude lay dying - "Oh, Gertrude, Gertrude, what is the answer?" Gertrude finally replied, "What's the question?"   Art needs to stay. God knows, Charley will need help with Savannah.   Art needs to find someone. I'm not too worried about Liz - she seems to be able to take care of herself, although she must get lonely. I wish she'd find someone, too.

I might come back as a Canadian goose. I know it's a Canada goose, but that sounds pretentious. I know my language must bug Art sometimes, but what's the use now of always watching what I say? I'm glad my women's group has labeled me *potty mouth*. Who would ever have believed that about me when I was younger. I never even used the f-word until I was in my thirties.

Art and I had always planned to take our pills when we reached seventy-five years old.   We just didn't see the use of staying around longer than that because so many bad things might happen after that - heart attacks, strokes, whatever. If we both could have lived to be seventy-five, we would have thought we had lived a long life, a good life, contributed something to mankind, and then departed in a death with dignity. We neither one wanted to end up in a nursing home. God forbid! I've worked in so many, and even the newest and best ended up being bad. I guess neither one of us wanted to give up control over our lives - or deaths. We don't believe in an afterlife and didn't want to be a burden for our children or anyone - yeah, right. I halfway thought Art might want to go early - with me - but I can't really see his doing that now. He's always been so damned healthy. Of course, so was I until the leukemia just sort of showed up suddenly.

If I just hadn't had the shingles - and its aftermath - the herpetic neuralgia, and the awful sinus infections, and then the asthma, and the skin cancers. If I just hadn't taken that toxic Campath - that just shot my immune system to hell. It's all been downhill since then, it seems. I did have some good years, though, even after I was diagnosed with lymphoma. I really thought I might beat this thing for a while there. I had over eleven years, and poor Barbara only had about nine months and practically no good days after her diagnosis, either.

I've got to go - I spilled Gatorade all over everything - my gown, the bedclothes. How did it even get in my hair? This is the second time that it's happened this week. Well, I sure put up one hell of a fight. I've got to go. "Bye, baby."

What I Did on Summer Vacation
(or in Lieu of Flowers)

This summer was the strangest summer of my life. Ann died in February, and I didn't know it at the time, but I felt sort of numb and also somewhat relieved that she didn't have to go through any more suffering. I missed her a lot - a real understatement. About two months later, when Spring was in full bloom, I felt awful most of the time. Friends, neighbors, people I formerly worked with - all invited me out - mostly to lunches and dinners. I accepted most of the invitations and was sincerely pleased that people were not forgetting me and that they were including me in some of their activities. For the most part, however, I felt like a fifth wheel. They didn't talk about Ann, except to say what a fighter or survivor she had been or how many years she had lived after being diagnosed, first with chronic leukemia and later with non-Hodgkin's lymphoma. I learned later many did this because they didn't know how I'd react, and their intentions were certainly good. I did talk about her until I was afraid that I was talking about her too much. I couldn't stop saying "we" instead of "I", or I kept saying that Ann and I had done this or that or thought this or that or discussed this or that.

I read some grief literature, tried to join a bereavement group and finally succeeded, as the leaders would not let anyone in whose loved one had not been deceased for at least four months. When I questioned the reasoning behind this, they said that participants would be too emotional or would miss sessions because they were still dealing with practical matters. No doubt this is true, but by the time I did join a bereavement group, I wondered if it was really the thing to do.

I decided to try to change my life and get everything in order. I had put off doing some repairs and things around the condo that I really needed to do, so I hired a handyman to come and help with about six or seven small jobs and paint a room. After getting these things done, the washing machine seemed to have sprouted a leak, although it didn't leak all the time. The dryer wouldn't dry clothes as quickly as it should. The hot water heater definitely had a leak that the first repairman thought was only condensation from the air-conditioner, which is in the same closet off the garage. I knew that wasn't the case and had the handyman come and replace the hot water heater. When he took the old one out, you could see where the bottom had rusted and it would have been only a matter of a few more days or so until it had gone through the metal enough to affect the bottom burner. There were simple enough explanations for the washer and dryer, too. I had been following Ann's directions from about six months previously when I had taken over all the chores around the house and instead of just pouring the liquid detergent into the washer on top of all the clothes, I had carefully held the cup under the incoming water, but I'd been holding it where it was splashing into the overflow drain, and thus there would almost always be a little water under the washer when it finished.

There was another simple explanation about the dryer - I had forgotten to empty the lint vent. Oh, I had thought about that being the trouble after a couple of weeks of forgetting about it and had wondered why it had not been as full anymore as it used to be. I even had the handyman look into it, and he took the vent tubing off and cleaned it out and made sure the outside vent was clear, but by this time there had been such a build-up of lint in the back of the dryer, that only a repairman from Sears could find the problem after taking off the back of the dryer and removing what looked like a ball of cotton candy that you'd get at the State Fair.

The point of all this is that you can prepare and repair and keep busy and clean and have things checked, and you still can't control everything - some things happen no matter what you do, or in spite of your best efforts.

I also had to have the cats that we'd had for thirteen years euthanized, for reasons I won't go into here. I had also essentially lost two of our best friends, one to a brain tumor and her husband to a memory disorder. While I took my first vacation in three years, two colleagues of mine at the hospital died; they were both only fifty-nine years old, and although one had been ill for some time, the other was exercising when his wife left to run to the grocery store. When she came back, she found him slumped over, dead. I jokingly told my relatives on the vacation/reunion in Florida that the first thing I did each morning was to have breakfast and read the obituaries - first to see if I was listed and then to see if anyone else I knew had died.

The vacation, except for the long drive alone down and back, was great. I had my own small condo right on the ocean, and both my sisters had large, three-bedroom condos that people could congregate in either for a meal or to play cards or just sit and talk after eating out at a seafood restaurant, as we did five of the seven nights I was there. I also rented a bicycle built for two and gave a lot of my relatives rides along the beach. We had a tent set up by

9 a.m. every morning where we would sit if we didn't want to stay in the sun all day, and then there was the sandbar where we would gather and watch a dolphin or two come into the deep cold water between us and the shore and put on a show for us.

Walks along the beach each morning were shared by from two to six relatives, and everyone got along well and seemed to enjoy being there and having me join them. It was a distraction for me that really did help, until at last, around 11 p.m. or midnight, I'd finally get back to my empty, lonely condo, and unable to sleep, listen to music I'd brought from home. In the car, I listened to compact disks and cassettes of music, all of which struck me as sad. Even the Bailey White short stories I'd brought, while witty and insightful, didn't cheer me up.

I've read books and pamphlets that were recommended to me, and they did help, but I've learned once again that you may not be helpless in a lot of situations and that it's how you view stresses and not the events or stresses themselves. Intellectually, I've always known this, and that keeping busy and planning what to do with the rest of your life or even on the next day may not work out - chance and unforeseen factors always come up, so you might as well try to keep up a positive attitude and laugh and not really care what other people may think because that's the way life is - Art's Philosophy Course 101.

One Stormy Night

It was a cold and stormy night in 1975 or so. It was in the twenties, and sleet was coming down; in fact, it was an ice storm. February in Indiana is often drab and overcast and rainy, but on this night, there was already snow on the ground and since all the trees were bare, they glistened in the wet, icy rain. It was a magical sight from the large bay window in our living room. Soon, the rain and sleet stopped, after coating all the trees in our neighborhood with wintry crystals, and the moon and even the stars came out and made it even more beautiful.

Ice storms are both beautiful and dangerous. The ice builds up too much and causes the limbs of the trees to break, making sounds like shots of gunfire. A really bad ice storm can sound like a battlefield, especially at night when the noise of the day has died down and there are sometimes echoes. Then we began to hear them - like rifle shots ringing out in the dark. It seemed eerie, as there was no one out. You could hear no traffic on the streets, and the only sounds were the clean cracking sounds - the limbs of trees breaking. At first, it was a good feeling, but then it began to be worrisome, as we wondered if any of the branches on our trees near the house were going to break off and fall on the roof or electrical wires. Craaaccck! - we would hear about every five minutes. It seemed as if a war was going on but we were in a safe place and just observing it from a distance.

Storms have always been attractive to a lot of people. There are those who like to ride out the storm, those who never want to leave when ordered to evacuate because a hurricane is on the way. Afterward, people always say they didn't realize that the storm was going to be so damaging, or that the shelters wouldn't accept animals, and they couldn't leave their pets alone. These may be excuses, though, because they want to prove themselves better than the forces of wind and rain and conquer their fears.

Storms are powerful and always change things. We weather storms, we say. But nothing is ever the same after a storm. We are bombarded with storms every day, most of them solar storms of radiation that we are never even aware of unless a powerful surge interrupts our cell phones or electric power.

If you had asked Ann when she was alive or if you were to ask either of my children if they ever remember a storm from childhood, this is the one, I am sure, they would mention. The beauty and the far-off noises went on throughout the night yet our home sustained no damage. Somehow we were changed by that evening, even if only a little bit, because we had weathered it together and because it added a little more beauty to our lives and memories.

Everything You Always Wanted to Know About a Mental Hospital

When I mention to people I've recently met that I worked in a mental hospital for over thirty-five years, I often get asked if I didn't get depressed working there. Years ago, before I retired, I got the same question, usually phrased as a statement: "That must be depressing." The truth is that it wasn't, not for me, and maybe only for a handful of others whom I knew.

What's depressing about observing someone come out of the depths of depression, or get a grip on their manic behavior, or be able to think more clearly, or stop obsessing about an imagined fault? What's depressing about reading a teenaged patient's mail to his parents, saying how he realizes that his parents love him or did things for his own good? Yes, therapists in those days read patients' mail. Even now it is okay if the patient is underage or on precautions. Most therapists would stop only blatantly delusional mail or letters threatening others that would be likely to get the patient into legal difficulties. Of course, back then the children and adolescents had parents whom they were involved with; now many of them are guardians of the state or foster children or teenagers who are not going back home to live but to another less restrictive institution, such as a group home.

The average length of stay for adults in 1961 was about ninety days; that's still the average stay, but there are many more patients at both ends of the curve - those who get out in ten to twenty days and those who are there for many months, partly because another placement in their home community can't be found. It was remarkable to see the difference in how someone had been acting upon admission and then later upon discharge. We had a grant for four years to follow up all the adult and adolescent patients after their discharge. Children (those aged five to about eleven) and adolescents (those from about twelve to eighteen) stayed longer, of course, because they were in school at Larue Carter - we had grades from kindergarten through 12th grade. One could graduate from Larue Carter High, but more often the credits were transferred to the high school in their home community where the diploma would be issued. We even coached older adolescents and adults who then received the GED. Most of the younger children stayed about nine months, while the teenagers stayed about six.

I watched lots of changes through the years in the treatment of patients - from being mostly locked wards (or units, as they are called now) to mostly open units and then back to more locked than unlocked. Nurses went from wearing white uniforms and shoes to ordinary clothes. Most psychiatrists wore ties but many of the others, psychologists and other professional and administrative staff, stopped wearing ties except on special occasions, such as when accreditation surveys rolled around. That's something else that's changed quite a bit. It used to be that we'd spend about six to nine months preparing for the once every three years' visits. We knew for weeks and sometimes months just how many surveyors were coming, and who was going to look at certain areas. We had researched their backgrounds as best we could and cautioned anyone who even thought of taking a vacation during their visit. Of course, the floors were spotless, most of the time, and anything that needed a new coat of paint was spruced up. Employees, even professionals, often had to be warned to complete their paperwork and have it in the charts and medical records on time. Raises, which often came only once a year under the state merit system, were often reduced or increased according to whether the employee's paperwork was done on schedule.

I heard that just the other day, two surveyors arrived in the parking lot with no advance notice and called the superintendent that they would be in the hospital in fifteen minutes and would be there for three days. Instead of spending time with each department head, such as in psychology, social work, O.T., medical records, dietary, etc., the first patient's name mentioned was picked to follow up. For example, they looked at the patient's medical record, seeing that the admission note had been in the folder right after admission and that a treatment plan was in the record within 24 hours, and that it was updated at ten days and then every thirty days after that or when any really significant incident occurred, that a dietary plan was there, noting any special needs, and then they went and looked at the living quarters and checked everything on that unit, even the contents of the refrigerator and its exact temperature, noting that no food items were in there with the medications. It makes much more sense to base accreditation results on such findings. And the findings and the resulting ratings are extremely important if the hospital is to get third party payments or Medicaid or Medicare money.

When I first got to Carter for my one-year internship, I went to what used to be called Chart Rounds, where the entire team met weekly, in a smoke-filled conference room for about two hours and reviewed each patient - as many as fifteen. Now the essentially same procedure is called Treatment

Review, and there is no smoking by any of the staff in any of the offices or conference rooms.

Mental hospitals are on their way out - most will be much smaller from now on, and most patients will be treated on a psychiatric or mental health unit in or attached to a larger general purpose hospital. The emphasis even in free-standing hospitals will be on trying out the many and various kinds of medications and adjusting their doses (this process is called a clinical trial, if the medication is still being researched), with a little psychoeducation thrown in. The latter term means educating both the patient and his parents, spouse, or other relatives about the side effects of the medications and the follow-up care. Follow-up services are usually mandated at one of the thirty-one state-wide mental health centers. These have a broad range of services, including an inpatient unit that functions like the mental hospital of old, but usually gets the patient out or into outpatient treatment in fifteen days, and almost never over thirty days.

Any new mental hospital today (and there are almost none being built any longer) will be very near or adjacent to a large medical center, because so many other medical diseases now mimic what people used to think of as mental illness. Another curious thing is that most psychiatrists don't do psychotherapy anymore, certainly not psychoanalysis, but only try out medications and dosages. They leave most of the therapy or counseling to doctoral level clinical psychologists or to clinical social workers.

I could tell you a few depressing things about mental hospitals, but it would be about the staff not the patients. As I've mentioned before, the way to tell the difference between the patients and staff is that the patients eventually get better and leave.

An Empty Canvas

I wonder if painters get their paints and brushes out and then sit and stare at a blank canvas? After finding notes and beginnings of stories in three different journals and trying to expand upon them, to no avail, that is, not being able to write more than a paragraph, I decided to sit down at the computer, turn on the Corel Word Perfect, and stare at an empty screen to see if any ideas would crop up. I'm grasping at straws, it seems - anything for an idea that I can develop into a memoir.

This isn't like writing a psychological report, where you have a structure - wait a minute, maybe I've latched on to something at last. Maybe I'll write a psychological evaluation of myself. Of course, there always used to be referral questions: Is the patient currently psychotic? Is the patient depressed? Is the patient delusional? What's his prognosis? What sort of defense mechanisms does the patient use? So, here goes.

Psychological Evaluation

Name: Arthur L. Sterne

Birthdate: December 10, 1934

Date of Report: December 1, 2002

Age: 67--just a few days short of being 68

Marital Status: Married

Examiner: Same as above

Appearance and Behavior During the Examination: Mr. Sterne appeared his stated age--pushing seventy, perhaps a little younger. He was dressed in casual clothes and appeared neat and well-groomed. He did not appear particularly anxious or depressed and, in fact, was rather personable and possessed a good sense of humor, laughing occasionally. He seemed to understand the nature of the examination and was quite cooperative, with a few exceptions.

Background: Mr. Sterne is currently retired, having retired the day after he turned sixty-two, six years ago. He was a clinical psychologist at Larue D. Carter Memorial Hospital for thirty-five years. He was one of a few state employees who took advantage of the early retirement package that let those with accumulated vacation leave use the money from those days to pay for his medical insurance until he reached 65 and could then go on Medicare. Actually, with the increasing cost of medical insurance, he was able to have enough money for the premiums for about 32 of the 36 months before he turned 65. He was somewhat bitter that the state saw fit to let him use only accumulated vacation time and not his accumulated sick leave, too, as he had approximately 102 days of sick leave. That just got erased unless he returned to state employment within a two-year period after leaving.

When asked about future plans, Mr. Sterne said that he thought he and his wife Ann would do some traveling, that he'd probably do some volunteer work, but not until after a period off of just not doing anything for a while. When asked what he enjoyed most about the early days of his retirement, he stated that he loved the fact that he didn't have to get up early, meaning that he could also stay up late, and that he didn't have to drive in rush-hour traffic. He also mentioned something about not having to wear a tie.

When asked what kind of volunteer work he did, he said that he never did actually get around to doing any, except for joining the Homeowners' Board at the condo community where he lived. He served on the board for almost four years, but it was mainly a thankless job. He did buy a computer and started to learn some of the basics, thinking that it would have been a big help in his previous job. He continues to attend his Tuesday night Scrabble Club and even attends the newer Scrabble club on the West side of town and even the club that plays in Avon. Asked if he thought he might be a Scrabble fanatic, he replied, "No." He mentioned that while he didn't view himself as extremely competitive, he did like to win and had picked up several trophies over the years. He also joined a Poker group and said he really liked to win at poker, even more so than at Scrabble, perhaps. When asked about other hobbies, he said he still liked to take nature photographs, and that he was getting more interested in people photographs, too, especially since the birth of his only granddaughter three years ago. He made a peculiar statement towards the end of the interview that I took as an indication of his wry sense of humor. He said that it was too bad you first had to have children to have grandchildren, but that he guessed that was the way nature had made things.

When asked about friends, he mentioned that he had also joined a memoir writing group and considered many of those in the group his friends. He said it was really difficult to be friends with neighbors and still be a conscientious member of the condo association board. When asked to be more specific, he declined.

When asked about his health, he stated that his health was actually quite good. Except for being slightly overweight and having a few allergies, he was fine. He said he'd just had appointments with the dentist, ophthalmologist, dermatologist, and family doctor, and that he guessed he was good for another year, at least.

When asked if he had any unusual or peculiar thoughts, he replied, "Yes, a lot." Again, he refused to elaborate. When asked if he had any concerns or worries, he asked how long the examiner had or did he just want generalizations? The examiner urged him to be specific, and he said that he often worried about money, his wife's health, his granddaughter's reactions to her parents' divorce, his son's divorce, his ever meeting his former daughter-in-law in person again, and liver spots. Other than those things, though, he felt he had few worries for someone his age. He didn't worry about life's passing him by or not accomplishing all that he was capable of, or of knowing the answer to all of life's big questions. It was just the little day-to-day things, like forgetting to switch the Clean and Dirty magnets on the dishwasher, finding at breakfast time that the milk had soured, thinking the dryer needed a new rubber bearing, being unable to get the new humidifier running properly, dropping the vacuum cleaner and having it gouge the wall in the stairway, and not being able to fit the new little thing-a-ma-jigger that had broken off the shower door handle - just everyday things like that.

Summary of Findings: Mr. Sterne appears to be a bundle of contradictions. He likes to be in control, is vain, competitive, somewhat materialistic, slightly obsessive-compulsive, and a relatively new grandfather whose characteristic ways of responding to stress are denial and minimization, just undergoing the normal consequences of there being only twenty-four more days until Christmas and nine days before being another year older.

Titles

You may remember that I said in one of my memoirs that I usually work from a title. I don't mean I pick a title our of nowhere and then start to write about it, but I may have a topic in mind and in some way I develop that topic or focus on part of the topic and then come up with a title for my memoir, before actually writing very much. Then, that allows me to keep adding sentences or paragraphs, if the writing is going well. If it isn't, I just end up with titles and very little else. These are some of the titles I was dealing with this past weekend, trying to settle on just one and write just on that. I had several starts on some of them, but none that developed enough to make into a single memoir I could read at the group.

These are some titles I was racking my brain over:

The Tuesday Night Scrabble Group is Always Odd, Even When Numerically Even

Absurdities of Daily Life

If I Won the Lottery

Neighborhood Characters

Motel Rooms

Brains and Eggs

Just One of Those Little Mysteries of Life

Whiskeypalian

Contradictions

Peggy Lee's Song, *Is That All There Is?*

The Best Advice I Never Gave

"*...And You're Innocent When You Dream*"

Indianoplace or Naptown

Two Carol Anns

Friends of a Feather

Nothing

So, out of all these titles, I finally wrote a little on some of them: Here's Whiskeypalian: I was raised an Episcopalian. I went to a church that was Gothic in design. I was even an acolyte. Usually I had to carry into the church either the cross or the American flag in the procession, which came up the middle aisle. Communion was only on the first Sunday of the month, at the 11 o'clock service, and then I had to help with the wafers and the wine, when parishioners came up and knelt at the railing in front of the altar. Everyone drank out of the same chalice, although it was wiped and rotated after each sip. The rector, as we called the minister, watered down real wine. All the wine that was blessed during the ceremony and not used up by the people receiving communion had to be consumed by the rector, the assistant rector, and the acolytes. It's a wonder they weren't called *alcoholytes* on some Sundays. There was always communion, but no sermon, at the 7:30 a.m. service, but I was, both then and now, not a morning person, so I never volunteered for that service.

Another title I got started on was Motel Rooms. Motel rooms are usually sanitized, functionally organized, with little natural light - usually heavy drapes over the one large window or set of sliding glass doors. Each has a bathroom, a vanity, a closet without a door, one of two reproductions on the walls, a trash basket or two, luggage racks, a large TV set, maybe a desk, and a table, with two chairs. The dresser will have a plastic tray with a plastic ice holder and glasses. In the better places, the toilet will have one of those little wrap-around pieces of paper to indicate no one has used it before your arrival. There is typically a large bed, or two double beds - the bare necessities for a traveler's life, on the road. The rooms all look alike inside.

We saw a movie once, *Dear Hearts,* where a woman was attending a postmasters'/postmistress' convention. The first thing she did, the character played by Geraldine Page, was to put out her own framed photographs on the desk and bureau. I always remembered that scene.

I'd better close for now and get started on my next memoir; I've already got the title, as usual - *The Meaning of Life--It Rhymes with Orange.*

Wind Sailing

I like to paddle a canoe, row a boat, swim, walk, ride a bike, and play horseshoes, and that's about the extent of my participation in sports. Not to sound too wimpy, I should say that I've participated in walk races, and I usually walk four to ten miles when I walk. I also ride from twenty to thirty miles when I go out on my bike. For some reason, I only play horseshoes on the 4th of July.

One year when I was about fifty-five, my daughter gave me wind sailing lessons at Eagle Creek Park. Since I usually only went there to rent a row boat or a canoe, I was apprehensive but game. I signed up for a late Thursday afternoon group and wasn't too surprised to find that the instructors were younger than my daughter. The other eight or so participants were all in their twenties, except for one man who was in his thirties.

We were told that if we didn't have a board (many had brought a brand new shiny one) we could pick one from among those usually used for rentals. One of the instructors, a summer employee, got us all together at the edge of the lake and told us how to position our feet on the board, coming around individually to show us exactly what he meant. He then gave a canned speech about safety. The instructor said that unlike today, most of the sessions would actually be taught in the water. It was a beautiful day with big white puffy clouds in the blue sky; the temperature was in the 80's, and there was a slight breeze. I thought to myself that it couldn't be more perfect for wind sailing lessons.

Some of the first people in the water had no trouble standing up on their boards and pushed off a little way from the shore. The others, including me, were given individual instructions and help. I was the last one, unable to get up on the board and remain standing more than a second or two. The instructor helped me repeatedly, only to have me end up splashing in the water. After numerous attempts, he said that they were all going out farther and that he'd have his assistant, a girl about sixteen, stay with me and help me. I attempted to follow all the instructions he had given me, but all my attempts were futile. I was getting a little embarrassed and fed up. Finally, the girl said, "Well, no wonder. You've got your feet positioned all wrong." She then instructed me how to place my feet on the board, but quite different from the way the other instructor had said, which I readily let her know. But, I tried her way and lo and behold, I managed to stand up on the board, which was a little wobbly, and then straightened all the way up, amid her words of encouragement. I then started "sailing" out across the reservoir. In fact, I kept on going, and the wind was helping a lot. Now the girl was telling me to turn and yelling instructions on how to do it, but I couldn't hear everything she was saying nor could I maneuver the wind sail. She then yelled at me to step off into the water or just dunk the board. But, I was windsailing, straight up and going along at a good little clip, and there was no way I was going to stop now on purpose.

I was sure I'd lose my balance eventually, but I just kept on going out toward the middle, then closer to the other side. Finally, a small speedboat caught up with me and yelled some more instructions, none of which I could execute, so I had to jump off. They insisted I get in the boat. One grabbed the wind sail and we headed back. So much for my wind sailing days.

You Just Can't Have Too Many Friends

Regina (she pronounces it with a hard g) runs two Scrabble Clubs in the Indianapolis area - one in Avon and one at Kessler Krest Baptist Church, which she and her husband founded about forty years ago. She's eighty-five and her husband, Hartsel, is ninety-two. He retired as minister about ten years ago, and his son Dan is now the minister there. Both Regina and Hartsel are still very active in the church, and she's an avid Scrabble player. Hartsel still mows their seven acres in Avon and occasionally mows the lawn at their old house on N. Kessler Blvd., where they always have someone who's down and out staying until he can get back on his feet.

Regina came to the Monday night Scrabble Club a while back, saying she had cleaned out fifteen feet of gutter because she didn't want Hartsel to get up on a ladder. She says she was persuaded to retire from her job in the accounting department of a large industrial concern when she was sixty, but she hasn't really slowed down in the last twenty-five years. She's been a secret shopper, testing out many restaurants in the metropolitan area, from the food to the restrooms, and getting free lunches. She and Hartsel own quite a few rentals, which she is always painting or redecorating when their tenants move. Her husband owns several side businesses, as well. Regina has run several very successful Scrabble Tournaments in Orlando in the off season, obtaining a complimentary wedding suite for herself and Hartsel for getting a large number of rooms rented. Her son in Florida has a radio program and, in fact, owns the radio station and arranges all sorts of prizes for the Scrabble winners, including free visits to Disney World. You'd be surprised how many freebies ministers and their wives get, at least to hear her tell it. They own a time-share in London and had owned one in Florida until they recently bought one out right. I've always thought of them as quite bright and caring and thought they were more sophisticated than one might suspect at first glance.

One evening at the Thursday night Scrabble Club, I arrived a little early, but Regina was there, having been dropped off early by her husband, as she doesn't drive at night anymore because of her advancing macular degeneration. We were talking, and she said she had a proposition for me and wanted to see how I felt about it. Evidently, the extended family, including a nine-year-old granddaughter, had been talking about *"The Rapture."* Her granddaughter appeared very concerned and had asked her if dogs went to heaven. Regina replied that they didn't - only humans went to heaven or wherever it was they were going in the seven years that all the Christians would be taken by God - or maybe just Jesus, I can't remember. The granddaughter looked worried and said that she didn't want to leave her dog when she left and wondered what would happen to it. Regina told her not to worry because she knew someone who was a non-believer and who wouldn't be going and would be around on earth for the seven years they would be gone. She told her my name and said they would ask me to come live in the pastor's residence - a very nice new house built way back off the street behind the church - and she would ask me the next time she saw me.

Now sometimes you can tell if someone is pulling your leg or not, but somehow I didn't think this was the case. I did say, "You're kidding, right?" But she wasn't kidding; she was dead serious. I acted insulted that she would think I wouldn't be chosen; after all, I was raised an Episcopalian and had been christened as a baby and then confirmed when I was twelve. Once you're saved, you're always saved, I said, or at least that's the way I always heard it said - not that I really cared about being saved or not. I, serious, but sounding as if I were kidding, said, "No way would I leave my condo and live in a parsonage. And I certainly don't want to take care of some little dog." She looked a little disappointed but went on to tell me that she and her husband had recently purchased crypts in the nearby cemetery, and that hers was on the top, as she wanted to be chosen before him, even if he had been a minister, since she'd been a minister's wife, which she viewed as being more difficult.

Other players were starting to trickle in, so we sort of ended our serious religious talk. I thought, "With friends like Regina, who needs enemies?" On the other hand, I guess friends come in all sizes, shapes, religions, beliefs, and just about every other characteristic you can think of.

A Man in Utah

A man in Utah was just convicted of bigamy - he had five wives and twenty-five children. Although he was a Mormon who believed in polygamy, he said after the verdict was handed down, he didn't really think he was legally married at all, having never obtained any marriage licenses; therefore, he didn't think he'd be convicted.

He must be a better family man that I am. I can't imagine having twenty-five kids. I guess there must come a point where one more just doesn't make a significant difference.

I learned at a high school reunion several years ago that a girl I had dated in high school had nine children. She'd been very attractive in her teens, but she never came to any of the reunions. I guess not. I called her up one time just after a reunion and found out that she owned and operated a day care business. Imagine that! I also learned she'd married a Roman Catholic and had four children in the first six years of their marriage. She and her husband then separated or divorced. Several years later, they got back together or remarried and had five more children in six or so years. You'd think people would learn. I never called again - just considered myself lucky.

Think of all the in-laws you'd have if you were married to five women at the same time. It boggles my mind. Think of all the birthdays and anniversaries, and dental and doctor and eye appointments. Think of communicating with five wives and twenty-five children. Think of addressing the Christmas cards and signing them - Merry Christmas from Art and thirty other people.

You'd certainly have to celebrate birthdays by the month only. Tax preparation time might be okay - one deduction for yourself and thirty for other dependents. You'd have to buy another van every six years - just to hold the new kids.

There'd be no such thing as an inexpensive family outing. "Let's go canoeing - let's see, we'll need sixteen canoes." On the other hand, if everyone chipped in a dime, you could rent a video.

Think what shopping at the grocery store would be like - thirty-one rolls of toilet paper, just so you wouldn't have to return to the store later in the week. Think about spending quality time with each child. If you could provide the basic necessities, it would be great. What about helping with homework? "It's midnight - better start making tomorrow's school lunches." Of course, they may all be home-schooled. I can see it now - the father telling the kids that they can't afford ballet *troupe* lessons. Or, one of the younger kids saying how they hate hand-me-down hand-me downs.

Of course, there may be some advantage - may *one* of the wives wouldn't mind ironing.

The Messenger

Most people are pretty patriotic, especially since 9/11. Watching President Bush on television try to rally the people into a united nation against terrorists, I couldn't help but feel he was sincere. We had been attacked in our own country. The people in the World Trade Center who went to work that day were innocent, or as innocent as any group picked at random from any place in the U.S. could be. It wasn't fair to those who were on the plane that crashed in Pennsylvania, either. Bush seemed to articulate the thoughts of the common people and become the leader that some thought he wasn't prepared to be.

In the months since then, however, I began to get a little more wary of where all this rhetoric was going, about the *axis of evil* and the calls for a regime change in Iraq. One of the reasons I didn't vote for Bush in the first place was that I thought he would lead us into another war. I think war should be the absolute last resort; it's sort of like my feelings about the death penalty. I'm against it in almost all situations, but there are a few where I think it might be appropriate. The Second World War seemed like the last good war, and I even question that, since I was too young to know exactly what was going on at the time.

I have been against wars when I didn't understand what they were to accomplish, or when I thought my son might have to go fight in a war. During the Vietnam years, I read two books that really helped cement my feelings and thoughts about the futility of war. The first was *Johnny Got His Gun,* by Dalton Trumbo, which told of a soldier returned from war and in a V.A. Hospital, who wakes up in extreme pain and then as the pain subsides realizes that he has no sight, no hearing, no arms and no legs, and then, almost panicky, that he has no nose, no mouth, no tongue, no palate. But he can still think, and the rest of the book tells how he devises a way to communicate with a nurse until there is to be an important inspection of the hospital and they hide him away so that the inspectors won't see him. The graphic detail is almost more than you can bear, but you have to keep reading to see how it turns out.

The other book was by, of all people, Mark Twain, who wouldn't allow it to be published while he was still alive. It was *The War Prayer,* and it finally was published many years after he died. It's sort of like a long poem about a patriotic nation, where people go to churches on Sunday and, led by their ministers, pray that their boys, their fathers and sons, survive and wipe out the enemy, and that the bombing raids are successful. One Sunday, after a sermon, a man appears who seems to be a messenger from God, who says before God grants them their wishes, he wants to know if they really mean what they have been praying for. He says that the prayer really has two parts - one spoken and the other unspoken. He puts the unspoken part into words and utters them so that all in the congregation can hear them, and then asks if that is what they want, to let him know, and he will see that God gets the message. When he tells this other side of the story, about the men and women whose bloody arms and legs will be strewn across their country's fields, where there will be starvation, where fathers and sons will not return home to their families, there is a hush in the church. The man had spoken quite eloquently, but when he finished, there was a pause, and then the people said that he was a lunatic because there was no sense to what he said.

All around the world today, in this country and in Paris, London, Berlin, and Rome, hundreds of thousands of people demonstrated for peace. All these people were not against war, although many of them were, but they were against supporting Bush. They thought we should wait longer and give the inspection process more time. They thought that we shouldn't go against the United Nations, whose Security Council voted against another resolution urging the use of violence against Iraq.

All of this is going on when another *axis-of-evil* nation, North Korea, is blatantly threatening to develop nuclear weapons. Is it really all about the oil in Iraq, and if it is, why do so many people not see it this way? Why can't there be more honest discussion about our real reasons for wanting to go to war with Iraq? Why doesn't the majority of people in this country see what is happening? As one news reporter put it, there are only about two exits left on the road to war.

Things I Know, or Think I Know, or Thought I Knew, or Who Knows?
Part Two

A – *Acting* - the best acting in years can be found in Clint Eastwood's movie, "Million Dollar Baby".

B - *Boxing* has the seal of disapproval from the American Psychological Association.

C - *Chocolate* has been found to be good for you - it releases endorphins, the chemicals in your blood or brain that give you pleasure.

D - It's all right to have *"Don'ts"* - just don't have too many of them, or they will limit your capacity for living life to the fullest.

E – *Ennui* - if it occurs in your life, you need to rethink what you are doing.

F - You learn more about yourself from your *failures* than you do from your successes.

G - I don't believe in *God* with a capital G or god with a little g or a life force or a soul after the body dies or whatever; it's tough not believing, but there *are* atheists in foxholes.

H - *Help* is often near if you ask for it.

I – *Interests* - have as broad a range as you can without embracing things just for others' sake.

J - Make a *jackass* out of yourself once in a while.

K - *Killing* any creature unnecessarily is wrong, so think about this before killing the next spider or ant.

L - *Like* is almost as good as love and sometimes better.

M – *Money* - as a friend and mentor used to tell me, "Rich or poor, it's good to have money."

N - It took me a long time to understand why a 2nd grade teacher insisted that *nothing* and zero were not the same thing (think of temperature, for example.)

O – *Opinions* - Don't be afraid to have them or express them.

P - *Petty* is a long, long way from pretty; you never want people to call you that.

Q - *Qoph* is a good Scrabble word to remember because you can play the q without a u (I know someone will ask, so here's the definition: same as koph - the 19th letter of the Hebrew alphabet.

R - *Read, read, read* - it's one of the most satisfying things you can do.

S – *Shortcuts* - there are hardly ever any.

T - If you have enough *Time* for everything, you've got too much time on your hands.

U - Try as you might, you can never *Undo* anything.

V - Never view yourself as a *Victim.*

W - *War* is always bad, even wars waged to maintain peace or right wrongs.

X - Sex is almost always *X-rated* in movies, while violence gets an R-rating.

Y - If someone in the South says "*Y'all*", he/she means "all of you" - more than one, unless it's a Yankee trying to sound Southern.

Z - I didn't know what a *Zither* was until I saw "The Third Man" and heard its haunting theme music played on a zither.

A Coalescence of Elements

It helps if you have an idea of a concept in mind when you start out to make photographs, or some would say, take them. That said, however, I've made many of my best photographs almost by chance - for example, seeing brand new blue silk tents at Washington Square for a huge car tent sale near dusk one evening as I was going to teach a psychology class at the mall, or driving by a place I'd driven by hundreds of times, but never in the fall on a very foggy morning - the side parking lot at Clowes Hall. One should be prepared by having a camera along at all times. I always keep mine in the car.

The photography club at the old Art League in Broad Ripple was aptly named - the Photo-Venture Club. It was like an adventure to start out with nothing but your camera and film and the task to take some photographs. You might have a filter or two or a wide angle lens, or some sort of prop. In fact, the only prop I ever used was a flower pot with artificial geraniums in it. Sometimes it would add just the spot of color needed, if I put it in the door or window of an abandoned house or church.

The monthly competitions each had a category - *windows, hands, red, abstract.* There was also an Open category, in which you could put any photographs you might have on any subject. Each month there were different judges from the community. They could be professional photographers who operated their own studios, high school art teachers, or artists in another medium who also did some photography or had a special interest in it.

For the most part, I thought the judges were fair, and they could usually articulate the reasons they had chosen to give a particular photograph a first or second place ribbon, an honorable mention, or no ribbon at all. The best judges usually went over each submitted photograph and made comments - generally about how it could be made better by adding this or deleting that. Once in a while, though, there were judges who had trouble making decisions or who waited too late in the week to spend much time on the task and would just put them into two groups - ones they liked and ones they "…didn't like as much," as if afraid to express their opinions. Very seldom would the judges be very critical of a photograph. In fact, saying nothing or very little was the ultimate insult, it seemed. Even though the photographers were supposed to put their names and other information only on the *back* of the photographs, some of the better known people had a style that was easy to recognize or their mats were unique. They might have done something special and/or peculiar to their photographs, such as tearing them up, and then sewing them back together or taking only black and white photographs, but adding pastel colors to various items in the photographs.

The thing I liked most about the club was also the thing I liked least about the club. It was the variety of approaches - relatively straight-forward shots to the other extreme where the technique seemed to overpower the content. The variety was stimulating to the others in the club, particularly the beginning photographers. It just so happened that I was a beginning photographer and a newcomer to the club at the same time, but this wasn't true of everyone. Some people came every Thursday night but never entered a competition; others came only when they had something to enter in one of the categories. Still others had been photographers for many years but had just started coming to the club meetings.

Some people took photographs of everyday objects; others put them in unusual contexts, either finding them that way or setting the scene up that way. For example, one woman took a photograph of a child's small red tennis shoe caught in some telephone wires; she also entered a photograph of a red, high-heeled satin pump out in the snow. Month after month her photographs looked as if she never left her house or yard.

I wanted to learn more about the techniques of photography - lighting, different F-stops, the use of different filters and lenses, and different kinds of film. It was rare to hear about these things, however, unless it was discussed in the critiques of the individual photographs.

When Ann and I went on photography jaunts, we just got in the car and headed out of town - to the countryside or some small town. Barns, churches, cemeteries, ponds, or something usual next to something unusual were often subjects. Occasionally, the color of something is what attracted me - a pink door with a powder blue frame to a tavern in a small town or a small series of storefronts painted purple.

At first I would be very selective when I found an interesting subject and take only a couple of shots of it. I later learned that the angle or perspective might make for an interesting shot. Sometimes I would take eight or ten of the same thing and maybe get only one worthwhile shot. I almost always knew, though, if not the exact shot, then at least the series of shots that would produce an interesting photograph.

Some say a photograph should speak for itself, but I think you can help by giving it an interesting title. I entered one photograph in a couple of contests as *The Little Red Truck,* and it didn't get even an honorable mention. When I called it *Detour,* it ended up winning several ribbons. Sometimes the title helps direct the viewer's attention to the element you want to emphasize. I had the same experience with one I called *Two Old School Buses;* I renamed it *Double-Parked,* and it won several prizes. A lot of photographers disagree with this notion and give their photographs only numbers, such as "Black and White, No. 3, 1985."

I did learn some good tips through the club meetings, such as don't put the center of attention right in the center of the picture, or that it is usually better to have something entering your photograph rather than going out of it. But I learned you can break these rules or guidelines sometimes, particularly if you can provide another element to the picture, such as a bright color to catch the viewer's eye.

Mats can make or break a photograph, too. When you first start out, you want to choose a huge variety of colors, often matching a color in the photograph. As you learn more, you see that it's usually best to use an off-white mat or neutral colors, such as beige and gray, which let the photograph stand out.

Often what attracted you to a certain scene in the fall of the year may look totally different in another season - either much more or less intriguing.

People, to me, are the most difficult to photograph. They always have expectations that may differ from you, the photographer. The best photographs happen when you have just the right coalescence of elements.

Outrageous People

Things aren't always what they seem. People aren't always what they seem. I had a professor once who said he could predict which students were going to be successful in graduate school in psychology if they mentioned somewhere in their application materials that one of the reasons they wanted to become clinical psychologists was because they were curious about people, what made people tick, act in certain ways, etc. rather than saying only that they wanted to help people. I've always been curious, especially about people. I used to love to sit in a railroad station and watch the people coming and going and wonder what they did and what their destinations were and why. I think it did help me in my job, and not just with patients, either. Of course, it spilled over into other areas of my life as well. Take my Scrabble Club members, for example. They're really a bunch of outrageous people. We start every Tuesday night's activities with someone's asking if we are odd or even, since we need an even number of people to play each of the three games in pairs. Someone always answers that we're odd, usually adding that even if we're even, we're odd. It's a joke that's old and a little stale now, but we've been saying it once a week since January, 1985, when we started the first official Scrabble Club in Indianapolis. Now almost fifteen years later, there are still many of the original members who attend. Most of the club time is spent playing and talking about words and learning new ones, such as *qursh, cwm, and tuque,* for example. But between games or before the matches start or when we see each other socially occasionally, one learns how interesting these people are.

George started playing in the club only sporadically when in Indianapolis visiting his brother here who was ill. George operated a Scrabble Club of his own in Chicago, where he had been a cab driver for twenty-seven years and where he lived in a rent-controlled apartment. He eventually moved here temporarily and stayed in his brother's apartment after his brother had to go into a nursing home. George visited him every single day. He told us little by little that his brother had worked at Lilly's and had never married, and his only relatives were George and George's daughter in Arizona. Time passed, two and a half more years, to be exact, and when his brother finally died, George said the amount of the inheritance was around a million dollars. Just about this time, the Lilly stock jumped and split or something, and the amount increased. Then, when they opened his brother's safety deposit box, they found a great deal more of Lilly stock and evidently some cash, so that George and his daughter ended up with a lot more than a million dollars. The only outward sign that George, who continued to bring day-old bakery goods to the Scrabble Club for snacks, inherited any money was the brand new fully equipped Dodge that he bought. The last we heard of George, who had moved back to his rent-controlled apartment in Chicago, was that he was building a home, a double-wide mobile home, on twenty acres just a few miles from his daughter's house in Arizona.

Rosemarie is a retired caseworker for the welfare department. She carries around two bullets still lodged in her abdomen from trying to defend one of her clients from domestic abuse. An irate husband shot and killed Rosemarie's client, and several bullets shattered one of Rosemarie's hands; two bullets eventually lodged in her abdomen where doctors thought it was better to leave them rather than remove them.

There are other members who absolutely hate to lose a game.   Others' behavior is almost as bad when they win. It's difficult to know which one is worse, unless, of course, both behaviors occur in the same person. Jubilation or whining are common in Scrabble players.

Now, if you're thinking these are some of the odd players, think again, because these are actually some of the more "normal" players.   Here are the definitions of the unusual words:

qursh--a monetary unit of Saudi Arabia
cwm--a deep, steep-walled basin; a cirque
tuque--a knitted woolen cap

Recollections on Being a Psychologist

I always enjoyed being a clinical psychologist. I can't believe that it's been over nine years ago that I retired. When I quit working, I decided not to keep my license current, as that would have required forty hours of continuing education every two years, and half of that had to be in workshops that were conducted by accredited people. Many of the workshops were out of state and cost quite a bit. I would also have had to keep my professional liability insurance, and that was very expensive as well. One had to keep an insurance rider for seven years after leaving practice anyway, just to be on the safe side.

I always liked to evaluate people, either hospitalized patients or clients seeking disability, because it was like unlocking a puzzle. I generally only had about three or four hours at the most to do any psychological testing, interviewing, and sometimes also interviewing members of the patient's family. Sometimes I had some referral information that pointed me in a certain direction, and other times I had very little history to work with. I always poured over the test results and looked for patterns and how these small samples of behavior obtained in a standardized way could tell all sorts of things about someone - intelligence, personality, signs of brain dysfunction, how a person usually coped or characteristically responded to stressful events. It was often interesting that someone would tell you more about themselves and their thoughts and emotions on questionnaires than they would just talking to them or even in a structured interview.

I also liked supervising psychology interns. Many interns, all of whom were earning a doctorate, couldn't spell well, even though they themselves had been to prestigious universities or private schools. Many professors let poor grammar and punctuation go, if the content in the reports or essays or term papers was exceptional, so often no one had corrected the student's mistakes. I had one very bright intern who couldn't write legibly and was one of the first to comprehend and use a computer. He had to write notes on his therapy patients after every session in the patient's chart, which would later become part of the medical record for that patient. What was the point of writing notes that no one could read, or that no one from the nursing staff was going to take the time to try to decipher? This intern went on to join the staff of another hospital in town and by that time had his own laptop, so he wrote all of his notes and progress reports on the computer and then put them into the chart or medical record.

Interns came with all sorts of theoretical backgrounds in terms of how they viewed a patient's psychopathology, but of course, the supervising psychologist very often had a different theoretical orientation. To me this didn't matter very much in the long run, because one had to write out directives and goals for the patient in terms that the patient and family members and other staff could understand. If using any particular theory to help them understand the patient was helpful, interns were encouraged to do so, but it was changes in behavior that could be measured that mattered. Even feelings and emotions in the patient could be rated, either by the patient or the intern/therapist or other staff.

Interns, for the most part, wanted specific suggestions from the supervisor to try with the patient, so often an intern would have as many questions for me as I had for him or her. Sometimes, though, one had to ask very open-ended questions to get the intern to be creative in terms of therapy.

Having an intern bring in notes or a tape of sessions was also very interesting because often what the intern said was being said or done was quite different from the actual tape. I always encouraged interns not to use jargon, but if they thought they had to, then use the term or jargon, but then go ahead and explain what the term meant and give examples; because very few people reading a report or evaluation were going to look up a specific word, unless of course, it had some sexual connotation. I remember the first time I ran across the term tricotillomania (compulsive hair pulling, often so severe that a person, especially a woman, might be almost totally bald) which I wouldn't have known without looking up.

Evaluations always had a format - starting with name, dates of testing, and what the referral questions were; for instance, "Does this patient show any signs of psychosis? or "Is this patient a good candidate for psychotherapy?" or "Is this patient likely to commit suicide or some violent act?" The tests that were administered were listed and whether an interview or other material gleaned from team or ward reports or referral material was used or not. Appearance and behavior during testing or an interview, findings and interpretations of the tests, and then the last and most important part - conclusions and recommendations - were also included.

Probably the part of the supervision that was the most difficult was the evaluation of the intern, done half-way through his rotation and then again right near the end. In later years, both the intern and the supervisor had to sign them. Luckily, I had been part of the committee that helped construct the evaluation tools and forms, and there were some very objective ratings. After finishing with the evaluation, the supervisor had to go over the evaluation with the intern and then submit it to the Internship Executive Training Committee. Most of the interns had come from highly respected colleges, most of our interns had been Phi Beta Kappa or had grade point averages in the 3.7 to 4.0 range (on a 4-point scale), plus recommendations from professors and training directors or former practicum placements that would indicate these were the cream of the crop. We also chose only interns who visited the center and were interviewed by at least three faculty members and then ranked them with all the other applicants, of whom there were usually about seventy-five or so to fill seven slots at the I.U. Medical Center.

I liked teaching Introductory Psychology and Abnormal Psychology at IUPUI, usually in the evenings and usually at Washington Square Mall or somewhere off the main campus. The students there were usually older, more serious, and not the typical undergraduate. I always thought I had to be fair in giving tests, so I used every type of question: multiple-choice where only one answer was correct, multiple-choice where all or none may be correct, true/false questions, matching questions, fill in the blank questions, short essay questions, and long essay questions where one could pick two or so from four topics. Sometimes I let students write out their reasons for choosing one or more multiple-choices or why something might not always be true or false. It was really more work for me, but I liked it better and thought it was fairer in the long run.

I even liked some of the paper work and the administrative duties that a lot of others didn't care for. I liked doing research because I thought that was where the most valuable information might come from. I could affect more than just one individual - maybe quite a few, depending on the results of the research. The only thing I didn't like was doing the statistical analyses of the research results, but now one can leave that almost entirely up to people who analyze research results on computer programs - people who do that for a living. And, of course, writing up the results of studies for publication wasn't something I liked to do - can you imagine that?

Brandy Alexanders

On the day before Christmas Eve about twenty-five years ago I had a kidney stone. Unless you've had a kidney stone or given birth, I've been told, you don't know what excruciating pain is. I thought it was a stone, but after being X-rayed, I was told by one of the resident physicians that no stone showed up. I had a call in to my family doctor at the time, and he called back and referred me to a urologist, who, lucky for me, was making rounds at the hospital and when paged, said he would be right down. Before even seeing me, he looked at my X-rays and diagnosed it right away, as if I didn't already know. He then came and showed me exactly where the stone was on the X-ray - even a lay person could see it. Evidently the resident had looked at the wrong kidney. When I passed the stone the next day, I told the doctor that I wanted it examined. He said that was done routinely, but it was probably just the garden variety. I told him I never wanted to have another one, and asked what I should do to avoid that. He said not to get dehydrated and to drink ten to twelve glasses of liquid a day - it could be anything - water, tea, coffee, soft drinks, whatever. So I followed his advice, which must have been good, since I've never had another kidney stone.

I like iced tea and soft drinks, ginger ale especially, but I don't think it's just the taste that makes something your favorite beverage. I think it's the circumstances surrounding your drinking whatever it is.

I remember going on long Sunday drives in the family car when I was a child and stopping at a filling station and putting almost my entire arm into an old-fashioned cooler with blocks of ice, trying to get the coldest bottle of Coca-cola I could find. I also remember drinking root beer in frosted mugs at a drive-in.

But I think the beverage I like the most - I even like the way the name of it sounds - is a Brandy Alexander because of the circumstances surrounding my drinking one. My late wife belonged to a women's group the last three or so years of her life - it was not the kind where one sat around swapping recipes or gossiping, although I'm sure some of that was done, but where important issues were discussed - whether there's a soul, or life after death, or the pros

127

and cons of donating your body (not just your organs) to medical science, and things like that. Each month where the meeting was held rotated among the members, but in December there was always a progressive dinner or hors d'oeuvres and wine at each house, and then they all ended up at our place last for Brandy Alexanders, which were more like milk shakes or desserts since we were the last house on the route. I never followed a recipe but everyone liked my Alexanders and everyone was always in a good holiday mood after having stopped at six previous places and having at least a taste of wine, if not an entire glass at each place. We didn't have to worry about anyone's driving home because all the women lived in our condo community and could just walk home - without worrying about the effects of my Brandy Alexanders.

Balancing Act

Author of a book at age 101, George Dawson didn't even learn to read until he was 98. He seemed to have a great philosophy of life, too. When asked the inevitable question about to what did he attribute his longevity, he said he ate anything he wanted, as much as he wanted, anytime he wanted. It was astounding how much his philosophy was like mine. He said he never worried because... "what was worry other than trying to control somebody else's life?" I'd never thought about worrying in those terms, but it struck a chord with me.

I've always done my darnedest not to worry and tried to get others around me not to worry, either, because what good did it do? I was reading a book the other day by the Dalai Lama, and he, too, said, "Why worry?" If something has a solution, there was no sense in worrying - one should be busy finding the solution. If it was something that couldn't be changed, then of course there was no need to worry about it, either.

I really think worrying is bad for your health. When I used to sit on the seawall with my grandmother and stare out at the ocean and talk, I really did enjoy that. But maybe, at least some of the time, when I was looking out at the sea, I was wondering where my father was, and when I was very young, perhaps wishing his ship would magically appear on the horizon. I didn't see much of my father because he was in the Merchant Marine and gone for months and months at a time.

"I'm going to throw myself in the St. John's River," we heard my mother say with a deep sense of helplessness as she ran out the front door, letting the screen door slam loudly. My mother was often depressed or anxious, and she suffered from severe migraines. My sisters and I were upset when she would leave like this, but then she would return, and we'd learn that she'd been visiting friends in the next block. We learned not to worry and that she would usually come back in a couple of hours in a much calmer mood.

Other days she might lie in a darkened bedroom with a damp washcloth on her forehead, all the shades pulled down so that no bright sunlight could enter the room. We learned to tiptoe around the upstairs and then go out and play. Instead of worrying, I said to myself that I'd grow up to be a doctor and learn to cure migraines.

My paternal grandfather shot himself at age 42, when my father was only sixteen and away at military school. I didn't learn this fact about my grandfather until I was a teenager. He was a banker who committed suicide because of financial reverses and who thought that his family would be better off with the proceeds from his insurance policy than with him. Unfortunately, he didn't know my grandmother had used the insurance premium money for other things and had let the policy lapse. This hurt my father, as he was the oldest of three and had to drop out of school and get a job to help support the family. That was fifteen years before my father married my mother.

Six months after I was born, my maternal grandfather died suddenly, so I really never knew either grandfather. Of course I had two loving grandmothers, and one of them, along with my two great aunts, lived to be in their nineties. When I was in the fourth grade, my parents divorced - for the first time. They remarried shortly but divorced again when I was a senior in high school.

Did all this affect me and mar my childhood? Well, yes and no. I was never very good at sports, mainly because I didn't know anything much about them. I was always the last to be chosen for most teams. In fact, if we were odd-numbered, often *neither* team wanted me. On the other hand, I was often one of the last left standing in the weekly spelling bees, so I thought it all balanced out.

As a freshman in college, I learned we would be required to take at least four semesters of physical education. I soon learned that there was a way not to let my poor showing in gym classes affect my grade point average. Students got so many points for attendance, more points for not being late, and then at the end of each semester we could get extra points for doing certain exercises that were supposed to tell the university how fit their students were. I found I could do the sit-ups and deep knee bends with ease and gain a lot of extra points. The first time I started out, even though I'd never done deep knee bends before, I just kept on doing them - up to about 250 of them. I didn't realize that I would hardly be able to walk up the stairs at the library for almost two weeks, but it was a small price to pay.

So although I may have had a lot of potentially sad events happen in my childhood, I developed a sense of humor and learned to laugh at life. I developed a sort of "bloom where you are planted" philosophy, but also always with the hope that someone would add a little Miracle-Gro once in a while.

My Life So Far

"Subtotals" was the title of a short story by Gregory Burnham that impressed me. It was in a book of *short* short stories that I was reading the other day called *Flash Fiction.* None of the stories was more that 750 words - some only one page long. "Subtotals" consisted entirely of categories and how many times the author had engaged in that activity or had those things or traits. When you finished, you had some idea of what kind of person he was. So I decided to write the same kind of memoir, but with different categories. Here it is:

Number of times born again 0
Number of traffic tickets received in lifetime 1
Number of traffic tickets thrown out of court and dismissed 1
Number of movies seen 2, 950
Number of cars owned in lifetime 12
Number of homes owned 3
Number of bikes owned 6
Number of days spent in hospital 4
Number of days worked in mental hospital 9,100
Number of Scrabble games played 2,375
Number of photographs taken 5,544
Number of photography contests entered 54
Number of photography prizes won 31
Number of dogs owned 2
Number of cats 15
Number of full-time jobs 1
Number of part-time jobs 9
Number of times tried to be a vegetarian 3
Number of times tried to be a vegetarian and failed 3
Number of books read 3,750
Number of days absent from high school 1
Number of religions tried 2
Number of unanswered prayers 342

Number of years a Christian 22
Number of years an agnostic 3
Number of years an atheist 42
Number of hats owned in lifetime 0
Number of jokes remembered the punch line long enough to tell 12
Number of states visited 27
Number of stairs walked up 89,758
Number of stairs walked down 89,738
Number of times fallen down stairs 3
Number of times fallen up stairs 4
Number of miracles witnessed 0
Number of insults--Given: 2,218   Received: 1,123
Number of times stuck scissors into electrical outlet 1
Number of miles mowed 1,283
Number of childhood home telephone 5-7755
Number of unfulfilled dreams 23
Number of musical instruments wished could play 2
Number of times attacked by dog 1
Number of times attacked by cat 26
Number of miles I'd travel to see the Pope 0
Number of miles I'd travel to see the President 50
Number of race walks started 4
Number of race walks finished 4
Number of job titles at hospital last five years of work 5
Number of *jobs* at hospital last five years of work 3
Number of trials testified at 1
Number of funerals attended 2
Number of weddings attended 3
Number of times returned a suit after wearing it 1
Number of waist size   Now that's where I draw the line!

A Taboo Subject

Most people don't want to talk about death or even discuss it. Most avoid it, like the plague. A look at it from someone getting along in years shouldn't be so hard to take.

Death is usually associated in one's mind with people we know who've died - people we cared about or, even worse, people we were supposed to care about but about whom we felt ambivalent. But death is all around us. Just pick up the newspaper, and each morning there is at least one full page of obituaries listing mainly local people who have died. That's another word people shy away from - many won't even use the word *died,* but will substitute *passed on* or *passed away,* or use some other euphemism.

What's so scary about death? I think it's either the fear of pain, which frequently accompanies dying and death, as well as fear of the unknown. No one has ever come back and told us about what happens after death, unless you believe in a celebrated resurrection or current psychics, who profess to be able to talk with the dead.

What's so horrible about living - and then dying? Most people in the world can't believe there's no hereafter - no heaven, no hell, no purgatory, no limbo, and no reincarnation - they just can't believe death is the end of life. Charles Panati has written that, "Our awareness of personal death may be the single most significant factor separating humans from other life forms." True, most of us would want to stick around as long as we could, if we were not sick or in pain.

It *is* difficult to imagine our not being around anymore, our ceasing to exist, but we can imagine all the other animals as ceasing a personal existence. Think how complicated it would be if we did go to a hereafter. Would we be a certain age? What if we had been murdered at age thirty, but our children lived into their nineties? Of course, there are those who say it is only the soul or the spirit that survives, not the body.

George Sheehan has written that the hereafter will be either a reward for being as good as possible or a punishment for transgressions in this life. Or, he says, one may be doomed to live the life forever that he/she has created on earth.

People always say, "I hope I live long enough to - " (Fill in the blanks.) But even if they did, they'd still not be ready to die - to leave. Except for the extremely depressed or the extremely deluded, life almost always seems worth living even under the worst of experiences. Think of the concentration camps. The depressed consider suicide because they can see no other way out. Did you know that it's on days like we've just been having, beautiful sunny blue-sky days, not too hot, not too cold, that the depressed find so hard to take, find so depressing? It's because there is such a contrast in the way they feel and the way the rest of the world looks - it's this discrepancy that they can't seem to tolerate.

People feel cheated if they perceive themselves dying young, or before a certain age, or before attaining their goals - whether their goals have been well articulated or not.

Can one practice dying? Maybe thinking about goals and reviewing your life can have a positive effect on how you live the rest of it. It's also a matter of control. People generally can't control aspects of their deaths, and it's this feeling of helplessness that causes us to want to avoid it. Controlling as much as possible may help - planning your will, letting children or relatives know your wishes for burial, services, etc. may provide some comfort, but it's really living each day to the fullest extent, almost as if it could be your last day that will prepare you for the inevitable - your ultimate ending.

There's no getting out alive. Let's face it, life is a fatal disease.

Things I'd Like to Do, But Probably Never Will

There's an unsolved murder of a woman physician in Indianapolis that I'd read about and always thought would make a great story, too. The first time I heard about it was in the *Indianapolis Star* , along with all the other still unsolved murders in this town. This one had a very interesting cast of characters.

It occurred long ago and involved two physicians, one a man and one a woman and his jealousy over their respective positions in the medical school. I even went to the *Star's* archives and poured through the headlines of the time. It seemed obvious that the murder was committed by the other physician, and he was indicted. The trial was moved to Greenfield so that an untainted jury could be found, but the jury there failed to convict him. The result was a hung jury. The woman physician lived in the Barton apartments - long since a downtown nursing home, now closed. There were many prominent doctors at the medical school whom a private investigator, such as me, could have interviewed for the resulting story.

Another person I always wanted to interview and write a story about is Jerry Hostetler, who owns the elaborate houses near Kessler, East Drive and Emerson Way. Anyone driving by is struck by the statuary in the yard, and one house just keeps getting bigger - added on to in all directions. Then the house next door was bought and also expanded and then a third house. All were then connected to the main house. I've only seen one brief interview in the newspaper, and it left many more questions unanswered than it answered.

Then, there is the guy Kiritsis kidnapped and paraded downtown and held captive for over sixty hours. It was his father whose mortgage company Kiritsis accused of shady dealings about a piece of land near Lynhurst Drive and Rockville Road on the west side of town. But the father wasn't there on the day Kiritsis decided to confront him, so he took his son, who also worked at the company. Kiritsis was found not guilty by reason of insanity and spent years in various mental institutions, but no one seems to have heard the full story about either this topic and the land deal or earlier situations in which Kiritsis was involved or in which Kiritsis' father was involved. Then, there's the judge who presided over the Kiritsis trial - himself the object of a long trial and later imprisonment.

What I would like, I think, is the investigative work, the interviewing of all the various people involved, the ascertaining of who was telling the truth, and what, exactly, the truth in each case was.

No Foolproof Formula

Mary once wrote about our memoirs group and said there was one person who, if he couldn't think of something to write, wrote about that. Well, self-effacing as ever, I'll try that again.

On a trip to Lebanon, Indiana not long ago, we visited Mason's Rare and Used Book Shop, a fascinating establishment, with a friendly proprietor. I sold a few books I no longer wanted and, of course, spent much more on some used books that caught my eye. One of them was, *Writing Articles from the Heart: How to Write and Sell Your Life Experiences* by Marjorie Holmes. It says that the things she longed to express did not come from outside sources or research, but from her own observations, reflections, reactions, convictions, and feelings. The book promises to help you write such articles, so I bought it, thinking it would help me write some memoirs.

One suggestion was to write an article on advice. I quickly rejected that idea, since it's been my opinion for quite a few years now that any advice given when not specifically requested, and sometimes even then, is like water over the dam. No one will heed it and may even resent your giving it. The second suggestion was to write a personal experience article. Well, I've been doing that. Of course, they should be memorable and adventurous, as well, she points out. First of all, I can't seem to remember any, and second, I'm not very adventurous. I've only needed a passport once in my life. Mountain climbing was something I never even understood how anyone could undertake; in fact, rowing a boat on Eagle Creek without wearing a life jacket and renting a pontoon on Brookville reservoir were my ideas of adventure.

Protest and controversy is another category, although she cautions that all the categories overlap. I've already written about the evils of war and the Bush administration. The last election results suggest that these things may not be as controversial as I thought they'd be. Politics might be interesting, but the closest I've come to being very involved was when I addressed 600 envelopes once for Birch Bayh's campaign back in the 1960's. I did attend a nuclear arms protest downtown once, but it was a sort of low-key family affair, and not too many people turned out on a grey, overcast day. I'd like to write about the influence of violent video games on the actual level of violence among teenagers and those in their twenties, but I don't really have any personal experience. It just makes sense to me that if the object of all the games is to kill as many of the players as possible and in the quickest way and be declared a hero at the end - and kids and teenagers spend hours and hours of their time in this fashion - that there just might be some violent consequences. Plus, the research literature points in this direction, but no one seems to pay any attention to it.

Essays and sketches are the next subject. She states that these should be based on observation, something I think I am good at and have practiced over the years, noticing even the smallest and most insignificant of details. I have written my views on polygamy, though in a humorous vein, and heinous acts done in the name of religion, and even customary rituals, such as wearing a tie to work; but the author says one needs to express something…"moving, significant, or lovely about the things we usually take for granted." I guess that lets me out - descriptive, sarcastic, ironic, insightful, maybe, if I try really hard - would be more like my writings, and that would be on a good day when my mind was working properly and I could remember a few things.

Nostalgia is another category that the author says has helped her sell her stories to *The Reader's Digest,*, *Better Homes and Gardens*, or *Today's Health.* I already wrote one with that in the title. Of course, my title was *Nostalgia? Nah--.* I spent about six lines pointing out things that no one will care about in the 21st century - cream on top of the rest of the non-homogenized milk in a glass bottle, Carter's Little Liver Pills, Brownie box cameras, double features at the theaters, along with newsreels, cartoons, and the March of Time, running boards on automobiles, rumble seats in cars, anything written in shorthand.

Maybe I could write a brief sketch on keeping trim and fit in your seventies - you know, sort of a science fiction piece.

The inspirational article, she says, is always something positive, constructive, and good. That sounds way too difficult for me to try to accomplish. The last suggestion is humor; now maybe I could attempt something in this last category. I guess I'll just have to come up with a topic I think is humorous for next time. Telling someone to write something funny is akin to telling someone to relax or be spontaneous - it just can't be done on demand.

Nostalgia? Nah--

Some things from the 20th century that we probably won't see in the 21st century: cream on top of non-homogenized milk in a glass bottle; tokens for a streetcar or trolley; Carter's Little Liver Pills; Brownie box cameras; double-features at the movies; newsreels, short cartoons, and The March of Time in theaters; drive-in movies; running boards on automobiles; rumble seats in cars; typewriters; anything written in shorthand. There must be thousands of other things.

After analyzing some of these, one may not become nostalgic about them. It seemed good to be able to scrape some of the cream off the top of the milk, but just think what this would do for your arteries, and then having to shake the bottle pretty vigorously to mix it up every time you used it, but hey! We should all be drinking one per cent milk or even skim milk at our ages. Tokens - who cares? They were more interesting than the usual coins, but who rides a bus anymore, much less a streetcar, except when we go to some exotic place or city in another country?

Carter's Little Liver Pills - most kids hated them, but they didn't taste bad; they were mostly candy and a little bit of vitamins mixed in, not enough to do you any good. Brownie box cameras - sure, maybe you learned how to photograph with them, but they were big and boxy, and you had to hold them very still; they didn't have a lot of the best features that are on digital cameras now - close-up lenses or ways to stop the action of runners or divers and get a clear picture. Double-features at movies - probably not, because a lot of movies are already over two hours long now. You can also watch as many DVDs in the comfort of your own home as you have time for. Newsreels and short cartoons - you can watch CNN or cartoons all day long if you have cable TV. The March of Time was interesting at the time, but sort of heavy-handed on the propaganda bit and usually expressed only one point of view.

Now, drive-in movies can't be replaced, because a lot of the time it wasn't the movies you went to see as much as a place in the dark two teenagers could neck. Running boards - they were fun, riding on them sometimes, but most cars look sleeker without them. Rumble seats - fun, too, but out back where you certainly couldn't listen to the radio or a tape - probably the convertible serves just as well for those who liked rumble seats.   Good old-fashioned typewriters - not as good as the new word processing that you can do on a personal computer.   You can go much faster, wipe out mistakes and never have to erase or use white-out; you can make graphs, change fonts and sizes of the printed words, use italics and underlining, and all sorts of things you could never get a typewriter to do nearly as easily.   Changing the ribbon always became necessary just when you were in the middle of something you didn't want to stop.   Short-hand - just ask any secretary if she really liked taking short-hand and then transcribing it - most didn't.

So before you get nostalgic, think for a moment at what replaced most of the things about which you may be nostalgic.   Nostalgia? Nah.

Cruel and Unusual Punishment

I'd been in at least four mental hospitals - working or being trained, but I'd never encountered anything like this. Even the 1948 movie, *The Snake Pit,* hadn't prepared me for this. Some of the men were wearing helmets and what looked like boxing gloves. I was told it was to keep them from hurting themselves. One man was naked; the others all had on generic-looking gowns or pajamas with no buttons or strings. I had to go thru this *day room* as it was called to reach the dining room that had been set aside for me to use as a temporary office on this locked ward. I was told to be careful of one patient sitting near a window because he would often spit on people as they passed through. Most patients seemed totally unaware of my presence, but a few were hyper-alert and stared openly in what I interpreted as a hostile manner. A couple of them yelled at me, calling me *"Doc"* and asking for cigarettes.

I was doing a pilot study for my dissertation research in 1963 and was testing patients at Central State Hospital in Indianapolis because I needed a group of chronic patients, as compared to the acute patients we supposedly had at Larue Carter Hospital. The attendant in charge asked if I wanted to stay for lunch; I noted it was only a little before 11 a.m. I declined. He said I'd have to wait until after lunch to use the dining room for my testing. When the food came not long after, I noticed that it looked like oatmeal or mush and some bread and that was all. The patients had only coffee to drink.

It had to be ninety degrees or higher, and none of the wards in this building were air-conditioned. Of course, at Larue Carter Hospital where I worked, only certain parts of it were air-conditioned. And hadn't I just visited the jail for some training and found that even the solitary confinement cells were not air-conditioned, and they were windowless, to boot?

What got me started thinking about this was a letter to the editor from a parent who was complaining about her child's having to stay in school longer this summer to make up for the snow days that were missed. She acted as if it were cruel and unusual punishment and even threatened to keep her children home while the temperatures were in the nineties. I guess it just shows how expectations can change one's entire perspective on things. No, I didn't walk barefoot through the snow to school when I was little, but I did attend public schools in Florida where the temperatures often got in the nineties, and we certainly had no air-conditioning. It made me wonder if this woman ever thought about mental patients or prisoners and the conditions they had to put up with. At the time, I couldn't wait to get back to Larue Carter, where my office was not air-conditioned, but where the patients were there for only three or four months, not years and years, and where they ate the same meals as I and all the other employees did for lunch. The meals were well-balanced and actually pretty good most of the time, and at least our dining room was air-conditioned. I guess it's all in how you look at things.

Thirty-five Years to Life

Most of the thirty-five years that I worked at a mental hospital I didn't find it depressing or any more stressful than any other type of job. If you were to walk onto one of the hospital units (they used to be called wards) you would probably see a bunch of men and women sitting around, most doing nothing, just sitting. If it was in the daytime nowadays, the television most likely would not be on - it wouldn't be considered therapeutic. Some of the people you would see would be talking to some other people - other patients or hospital staff. The staff would not be identified by uniforms, since uniforms went the way of wards. If it was a locked unit, meaning that you had to have a key to open the main door or you had to ring a doorbell and someone had to let you in, then anyone with a tie or belt would likely be a staff person, usually a psychiatrist or a psychologist. The patients on that unit wouldn't be able to have those items, not only for their safety but for the other patients' safety, as well. Ties and belts are considered items the suicidal person might try to use, although I have only heard of two or three attempts to hang oneself with a belt in all those years. You hear of that more in jails.

There's an old joke about a patient welcoming a new patient to the unit and asking him if he knows how to tell the patients from the staff. He tells him that the patients eventually get well and leave. There's certainly a lot of truth in that joke, believe me. Patients for the most part have the same difficulties in living or coping that the rest of us have. For some reason they just haven't coped very well. Their brains or biochemistry may be just slightly different, perhaps, from the average person's in that they may have more anxiety or depression that accompanies their actions or thoughts, or, occasionally, their thoughts may be stranger than the average person's. But I know a lot of so-called average people whose thoughts are really strange, even incomprehensible. Some patients may see or hear things that other people don't see or hear, or at least the others don't talk about them if they do. But again, I've known people who saw little people or figures in raindrops or heard voices that others didn't at some point in their lives or under certain circumstances, such as a great deal of stress, or grief, or under the influence of alcohol.

Sometimes what determines whether a person gets into a mental hospital rather than an outpatient clinic is the incompetence of the therapist or a series of mishaps or factors such as lack of money or power. Sometimes that keeps them from going to jail rather than a mental hospital, too. Whom the person knows, or which agency, either mental health or corrections, got involved with the person first may determine where he or she winds up.

A long time ago, in a rather naïve effort to get this point across, I arranged for my abnormal psychology class at IUPUI to visit our teaching hospital. After a tour, I interviewed first an inpatient and then a social worker in front of the class. Even though the male patient was dressed more casually and not as well-groomed as the social worker (who was interviewed as if she were a patient) they both told the truth when answering my questions, some of which concerned problems they had experienced and why they were at the hospital. The female social worker looked slightly angry at times and occasionally stared at some of the students, but for the most part their behavior was quite similar. The class voted almost unanimously that the social worker was the more disturbed of the two and that she would be more difficult to work with. She was a well-liked, competent social worker and didn't exaggerate the difficulties of problems she had gone through in her life. The patient, for the most part, was not overly anxious or depressed and, in fact, had been a graduate student in physics at a large, well-known university before attempting suicide in a rather bizarre way. Stereotypes entered into the students' opinions a great deal. None of them seemed to think that "…there but for other circumstances, go I." The surroundings really did color their thinking.

After thirty-five years at a mental hospital, I was finally discharged - I mean, released - no, able to retire.

Now or Never

I thought I'd just sit down at the computer and see what flowed out of my brain onto the blank page, and since I always work from a title, that title just popped into my head. Now what does that mean? Can I write an entire memoir with that title? What will the content be? I'll just see what inspiration comes as I sit here.

Well, just as some sort of thought was about to gel, the telephone rang. It was my son, Charley, saying he had picked up Savannah in Bloomington and they had just arrived home, as the traffic had been awful, with the interstate down to only one lane in some places. We decided to meet at the MCL Cafeteria on West 86th St., as Savannah loves to get a drumstick there, along with mashed potatoes and green beans. In fact, she gets the same thing almost every two weeks when we meet for lunch. Evidently, it's the only time she gets fried chicken, which she likes a lot.

It looked sunny outside, but scattered thunderstorms had been predicted. In the summer in Indiana you have to plan mostly by looking at the sky and not depend on weather forecasters' predictions. We planned to go to the Talbott St. Art Fair after lunch - maybe let Savannah get her face painted or something like that. Then we thought we might go down and rent a paddle boat on the canal. I'd bought two books at a garage sale for her and also a toy rubber snake that looked so real that I hadn't been able to resist getting it at the same garage sale several weeks before. Now Savannah and I have to figure out a way to plant it in the front yard so that Charley will encounter it when he is working in the yard. She loves to play tricks on her dad and of course I'm a willing participant.

Charley works late at Some Guys on Friday nights, and he has to get up early every other Saturday to drive to Bloomington to get his daughter; he has her Saturday through Monday every other weekend, but that will probably be shortened when she starts kindergarten in August. Anyway, they both always need a short nap between about 11:30 AM and 12:30 or so, and then we meet for lunch at 1 PM. Savannah seems to like the routine and when we change it very much, she lets us know she doesn't like it one bit.

Savannah turned five last Christmas Day. She's tall for her age, and grandpa thinks she's brighter and smarter than the typical five-year old. Her language reflects that she lives with her mother and a half-sister who is fifteen. She's learned to roll her eyes and say, "Whatever" with a nonchalant air.

I enjoy these outings with them, and in the past we've been to many of the usual places one takes children this age. We're waiting until the lines diminish at the dolphin exhibit at the Zoo, but that will be coming up soon, I'm sure.

Jenny, Charley's ex-wife, told him on his answering machine the last of the week that she may not be able to pick Savannah up on Monday afternoon, because her car was making strange noises. While this may be absolutely true, Jenny seems to have a lot of excuses. This time Charley had a very important meeting to attend on Monday evening that couldn't be changed, as it is his only day off except for the weekend days he has Savannah's visits. He's learned to deal with Jenny in a very matter-of-fact way that seems to bring the desired results. He told her that he wouldn't be able to bring her back to Bloomington until later on Monday night but that maybe Jenny should borrow a car from some of her relatives in Bloomington and get Savannah at the previously agreed upon time. Jenny called back and said she'd arranged to borrow her parents' car. Joint custody isn't all that's it's made out to be.

Where that title comes from, I have no idea - it must have meant for me to sit down and write a memoir *now or never* is all I can make of it.

Larue D. Carter

I worked at Larue D. Carter Memorial Hospital for over thirty-five years. I had never heard of the man for whom the hospital was named, but it seemed a good place to take an internship way back in 1961. I would be exposed to acutely disturbed patients with good prognoses, and all ages, from children as young as four to adults in old age. There would be inpatients and outpatients and a chance to do research and teaching. I would get to hone my skills in individual psychotherapy as well as group therapy and even psychodrama. The average length of stay for an adult inpatient was ninety days, which was considered a short stay in those days when many patients were sent to large state hospitals with not very much hope of getting out for years.

Upon entering the lobby, one saw a very large, almost life-size portrait of a very distinguished-looking man – Dr. Larue D. Carter. Only a few of the people who worked at the hospital seemed even remotely interested in or curious about who Carter was, except for the obvious fact that he had been a pioneering psychiatrist in Indiana.

Through the years I learned tidbits of information about him and finally was able to gather some interesting facts about his life. Carter's full name was Larue Depew Carter - Larue is spelled with small letters - no capital R as many people like to write, especially *The Indianapolis Star*. Family members and close friends called him "Ruey" or "Rue - that may be the origin of capitalizing the "r".

He was born in Westfield, Indiana on March 17, 1880 into a Quaker family and attended Quaker school. He graduated from the Medical College of Indiana (later merged with the Indiana University School of Medicine) in 1904 as class valedictorian. He interned at the Indianapolis City Hospital (now Wishard Hospital) from 1904 to 1906 and then became a surgeon for the Tom Boy Gold Mining Co. in Colorado 1906-1907. Carter then moved to the Eastern Indiana Hospital for the Insane (now Richmond State Hospital) where by 1912 he had become the assistant superintendent. From 1912 to 1914 he took a residency at the Philadelphia General Hospital and did graduate work in neurology and psychiatry at the University of Pennsylvania School of Medicine, before returning to Indiana to go into private practice.

In 1916 Carter entered the Medical Corps of the United States Army where he remained in service until 1919, at which time he held the rank of colonel. Also in 1916, he married Anna May Gant, a City Hospital nurse, from Nineveh, Indiana. They never had any children. Carter was mildly hypertensive at age thirty and developed a markedly elevated blood pressure in middle age, for which there was no effective treatment at the time.

Associates say there couldn't have been a better role model as a physician than Dr. Carter. He saw relatives and did his own social histories. He often went to the hospital to see relatives on Sundays when they were visiting a patient. He was known as a born teacher. He wrote at least twenty-eight scientific papers, all in longhand, since he didn't type. For many years Dr. Carter operated the Norways Hospital, located at 1200 East 10th St., and lived in Woodruff Place before he moved to a residence at 4280 N. Meridian Street. Just south of the Carters was the residence of Booth Tarkington, the Hoosier author, who is said to have written to a friend that, "I sleep peacefully at night because three of Indiana's better physicians' homes can be seen from my bedroom window. I hope at least one of them still makes house calls."

When Carter died in January, 1946, of a cerebral hemorrhage, plans were being made to build a state teaching and research hospital adjacent to the I.U. Medical Center. It was to be a place where all the other state hospitals could send their staff for training. Ground was broken in 1949 and the hospital opened in 1952, admitting its first patient July 28, 1952.

The portrait of Larue Carter which hangs in the lobby was done by the artist Wayman Adams, a fellow Quaker who had known him prior to World War I. The artist agreed to do the painting primarily from two studio photographs, but when it was almost near completion, Ann Carter thought the expression on his face was too grim and Adams altered it. Ann placed a single red rose in a vase in front of the portrait on his birthday every year - a practice Dr. Reed and his wife continued into the 1970's. Dr. Philip B. Reed and his wife were adopted by Ann Carter after Larue Carter had died, even though they were adults at the time of the adoption. Dr. Reed had married the adopted daughter of Albert E. Sterne, M.D. (unfortunately, no relation to me, even though his name was spelled the same, with an –e on the end) who founded Norways and had been responsible for hiring Dr. Carter many years earlier.

Carter is buried in Crown Hill Cemetery, but his portrait still hangs in one of the lobbies at the hospital, which has moved to the Cold Spring Road location of the old V.A. Hospital. A new Carter Hospital is being planned nearer the I.U. Medical Center or Methodist Hospital, but it is uncertain if it will carry the name of Larue D. Carter, truly a visionary in his time.

Of Mouses and Men

When I learned that *mouses* was a new acceptable Scrabble word, I thought I should really learn more about computers. All the jargon coming from the computer field made all the psychiatric jargon I had been used to all these years seem tame by comparison. Besides, as a psychologist I almost always tried to refrain from using a lot of jargon and to explain things in laymen's terms. Not so with computer experts! When my son Charley and I went looking for identical computers, it was because I wanted to get the exact same kind as him, thinking that when I had problems or questions, I could just run them by Charley and know what to do to fix the problems. Wrong! Anyway, you have to know how many gigabytes of hard drive you need, what software is, what speed you want for your modem, what a bubble jet printer is, etc. just to be able even to talk to the computer salesman at the store. Computer salesmen and technicians all seem to be nineteen years old or younger and with enough arrogance and condescension to make any lawyer blush.

One of the first questions they ask, of course, is what do you want to do with the computer. Well, if you're old enough to know what Walnettos are, you won't be able to answer that question. Of course, I knew I wanted Windows in a fairly current version, not even knowing at the time just what Windows was. We ended up getting two computers with a great deal of software included free of charge, a Canon (I recognized the name of the camera company) color bubble jet printer, and a monitor (why couldn't they just call it a screen and be done with it?) Luckily, Charley installed his first and then being grateful I had helped him pay for his, came over and I would say helped me install mine, but he really installed mine while I watched and tried to observe what he did - everything going at about twice the speed for me to get even a clue as to what was happening. Then, of course, I wanted to get e-mail, which meant I had to sign up for Internet Service.

I did end up taking a class that explained some of the computer's functions and terminology. I don't know why the computer can't be programmed to tell you that you've just made a mistake, and what you need to do to correct it; but instead, of course, it gives you messages saying something to the effect that you've performed an illegal operation, making you wonder if somehow, just by laying your hands on your keyboard, you've done something awful for which you might get sent to prison for life without parole. Then you get other messages, telling you that Autoexe. cannot be run or that your formatting is incorrect or that the message you tried to send has been sent back as *demon mail.*

I used to have fun going to the Library Society Book Sales, picking out new fiction or biography, but now I have to find *Windows for Dummies* or *Computers for Idiots.* Then when I get them home, I find that my screens never look the way the diagrams look in the books, or the messages are totally different and I'm just as in the dark as I ever was. It even makes you question your intellectual capability or perhaps makes you think that you really are too old to learn new tricks. I paid for a five-year warranty that covered everything, thinking this, for once, would be worth the money involved. To use the warranty, though, you first have to talk with a technician at an 800 number. He remarks that "… with an old computer like yours"—"Wait a minute, I tell him." My computer is only two years old ! He apologizes, somewhat, and says that it is just standard usage to refer to any computer and accompanying hardware as old if it is over a year old, and that I shouldn't take it personally. I plead senility regularly just to get him to tell me the instructions more slowly.

I finally catch on and get the name of the technician and ask for him personally when I call back, only to be told that Kevin or Todd or Brian could refer to many of the names of the computer techs and that I don't have to do that because any technician can just bring up the information on the computer screen and know not only what my original complaint was, but also what each person before had told me.

I gradually get more competent and understand some of the terminology and feel more confident, especially in some of my usual tasks, but then I have to learn to attach something to my e-mail messages, or I have to download a large color photograph. I've had a scanner that I got last Christmas that I still haven't used. For a while I got competent enough to play Scrabble with players in Australia and Japan and to play e-mail Scrabble with six people each day, until one day I found I was unable to play at all because my Scrabble CD has become contaminated or something to that effect. Then, I was told to Uninstall the Scrabble CD and reinstall it. Of course, it won't reinstall. I find others are having the same problem and I learn that the CD says, in very fine print, that it is only good for about one year from date of purchase, and no new CD's can be bought.

I'm going to try to make our Christmas cards this year on the computer. I've already bought the special paper and envelopes. I've picked out a photograph that I made while in Savannah, Georgia, last year. The technician at CompUSA said a child could use the Card Making kit - it was that easy. I've read the directions twice and consulted two friends about how to go about just changing the print from black to green for the greeting, and so far I've almost had the courage to unwrap the software. Oh, well, there're still forty-five days until Christmas.

Sexy, Provocative, and Risque

No, my memoir isn't going to be any of those things mentioned in the title. Those adjectives belong to the memoir Shari read to the memoirs group at our last meeting. You remember, the memoir about clothes-optional resorts and skinny-dipping. I've been worried the entire last two weeks about this last meeting of the year for the memoirs group since it's being held at Shari's home with a swimming pool. Now I love to get some sun and cool off in the pool on a warm summer's day, and that's where you can find me many weekdays during the summer - sitting around the pool at our clubhouse. I usually don't go on weekends, as it is more crowded then, and the people all seem to be younger and have bodies that can stand up to the scrutiny of others' stares. I don't have that kind of body - certainly not the kind of body that I'd want to skinny-dip in at this late date. Of course, it wouldn't be called skinny-dipping at all - maybe fatty-dipping or something like that.

With the exception of our hostess, who has already racked up quite a bit of experience in this sport, if you are to believe her memoirs are anywhere near the truth, even as she remembers events and how they actually happened, I doubt any of the others in the group would want to skinny-dip, either. Several members might not look bad in bathing suits, but I don't know about *in the altogether*. I thought maybe I should bring my camera along, as I wouldn't want to miss any human interest photographs for the State Fair competition in August. I heard two people say that they weren't even going to think about going swimming - in a suit or not. It's been so hot and humid the past week, though, that a refreshing dip in a nice pool midday seemed very inviting.

I went to the Talbott Street Art Fair on Saturday with my granddaughter and son. We went through quite a shower on the way there, but just as we found a parking space near one of the entrances, the rain stopped. We then walked through crowds for the next hour, and the humidity made it seem like a steam bath. We came upon a booth described as having *Fun and Funky Folkart* that had funny little sayings painted on small pieces of wood, suitable for hanging. I just couldn't resist buying our hostess one of the plaques that she may be able to put up somewhere near the pool area in memory of a visitor - whom the saying describes perfectly (if I had even thought of skinny-dipping, which I hadn't) and it says, "I don't skinny-dip…I chunky dunk."

Tony Kiritsis

(Or Testing My Most Famous Patient)

It was a Thursday night, and I was playing poker on the west side of Indianapolis with a group of men, most of whom worked at the hospital where I was employed, when several of our wives called and told us about the continuing incident happening not far from where we were and that was being broadcast on all the TV stations. It was February, 1977. Our host immediately turned on the television, and we interrupted our game to watch the drama being played out on the screen - a deranged-looking, foul-mouthed desperate man leading another man around whose neck was wired to a shotgun that the kidnapper said could go off at his will. Although Kiritsis said he would only talk to a local radio newscaster, Fred Heckman, to get his story out and to negotiate the release of mortgage executive Richard O. Hall, he was doing a lot of talking anyway.

Kiritsis held Hall hostage for sixty-three hours in Crestwood Village West, an apartment building just blocks away from where our poker group met. I might have watched a little longer if I had known at the time that I would have to administer psychological testing to him and come to an opinion about his sanity. The evaluation by the hospital staff was done at the judge's request as a "friend of the court," and my testimony would be a matter of public record, although most of what I would say at the trial or in this memoir had already been in one of the local newspapers or carried by television newscasters.

His trial and subsequent finding of not guilty by reason of insanity resulted in eleven years of stays in three different state mental hospitals: Larue Carter, Central State, and Logansport. The laws regarding insanity, a legal term, were changed because of what happened in this notorious case. Now someone in the same situation would be able only to plead *guilty but insane* or guilty but substantially not able to determine right from wrong or to control his acts. A not guilty verdict would no longer be a choice, under the circumstances. The events were captured on television for posterity, so there was no denying they took place. Kidnapping, of course, is a federal offense, a fact Kiritsis seemed to ignore.

Kiritsis was eventually given a draft for five million dollars (it was phony, of course) and offered immunity from prosecution if he would let Hall go unharmed; this too was fraudulent, as were so many self-fulfilling prophecies, in the case over a period of years.

Actually, every professional who interviewed or evaluated or tested Tony before his advisors had him plead not guilty by reason of insanity, thought that he was not mentally ill currently and most likely not so when he committed the crime. All the professionals who saw him after it was learned that his plea would involve insanity as a defense were uniformly on the side declaring him mentally ill. After the jury found him not guilty by reason of insanity, the judge, Michael T. Dugan, ordered him held by the State Department of Mental Health until psychiatric examinations found him suitable for release back into society. Kiritsis wouldn't submit to examinations, and he ended up spending eleven years in various mental institutions, until finally agreeing to be evaluated in 1988 by a psychiatrist not affiliated with the state in any way. A memo later turned up from a high state official telling the psychiatrists at Larue Carter Hospital to find Kiritsis mentally ill and thus keep him hospitalized.

Tony came from a family of Greek origin. It was rumored that his father had murdered another man to get his passport to use in immigrating to the United States under a false name. Tony said his father was very cruel and used all sorts of verbal and physical punishments on all his male children. Tony himself had used the same tactic that he used in 1977 years earlier when he had held his sister, Effie, at gunpoint in her trailer in the family trailer court for a weekend, until she finally agreed to give him the sum of $55,000, part of an inheritance. It was this money, along with the loan from Meridian Mortgage Company, that he used to buy the land near Lynhurst Drive and Rockville Road that he planned to develop into a shopping center. In fact, Tony had used his anger many times in the past to get what he wanted and had even been arrested for threatening to kill his brother at one time. He always managed to get out of these situations eventually without ever going to prison, so you could say he had practiced this crime many times in the past and had been successful.

Tony referred to himself as a national hero, and a lot of people in Indianapolis agreed that he was the little guy being cheated by monied interests and that he was fighting for his life. The trial had a lot of characteristics of the later O.J. Simpson trial, except that Tony had not actually killed anyone and in fact had let Hall go without injuring him, except for perhaps causing mental anguish.

A few other interesting tidbits: one woman in the jury appeared to be asleep while I gave my testimony, late one afternoon. On another day Tony's brother Jimmy performed the Heimlich maneuver on the judge's bailiff, who was choking on a piece of meat and turning blue in the City-County cafeteria. The judge during the trial, Michael T. Dugan, was several years later involved in a big scandal and fraud and ended up spending years in prison himself. The mortgage company did foreclose on the property after Kiritsis was being held in a mental hospital and, no surprise, really, ended up getting the property in a sale for which there were no other bidders.

All the local media people, columnists, such as Freemont Power and Tom Keating, and TV newsmen like Jim Cochrun and Mike Ahern, wrote or reported about the case over many years. Even *Newsweek* in an article devoted to the events that characterized the 1970s included Indianapolis for the event which they characterized as terrorism. It also changed the way the media covered high profile situations. Today they probably wouldn't agree to a kidnapper's demand that he be televised all over the country. One local photographer did get a Pulitzer Prize for his photograph of Kiritsis that was shown around the world.

Years later, just after Kiritsis was discharged in 1988, he sued one hundred and one people - almost all the people who had had any part in his long stay in three mental hospitals, Larue Carter, Central State, and Logansport, but I was pleased and a little puzzled that I had not been included in the one hundred and one people listed.

Trials and Tribulations
Or How to Manage Information Overload to Make One's Life Easier

It's reported that there is a tremendous increase in Alzheimer's Disease, in part because more people are living longer than ever before. I think part of the problem is that there is more to remember now. I mean, you have to know your home telephone number, maybe a business telephone number, and now a cell phone number. All these numbers include ten numerals. When I was growing up, most telephones had only five numbers, and my parents had only four numerals in their telephone number. One also has to remember his social security number and be able to rattle it off quickly. One has to remember the code numbers to access the bank machine. There's our address, too, and perhaps a garage door opener number, our bank account number, telephone numbers of relatives and friends. Of course, there are all sorts of other numbers that we have access to by means of cards that we carry in wallets or purses - such as a Medicare number, driver's license number, etc. Nowadays, one has to know all sorts of passwords to access their computers or websites on the Internet or various software programs.

Because of all this mass of numbers in our brains, I think it is more of a retrieval problem than a memory problem. We just have so much more stored in our sixty, seventy, or eighty-year old brains than the average twenty or thirty-year-old.

In January I got a new computer; in June I got a new digital camera; in September, I got a new cell phone. I already felt technologically challenged, but with all the devices on these new instruments, which are all made to make your life easier, I find it hard to cope and keep up with everything. I learned to make labels on the computer this past weekend; once you know how to do it, it's really quite easy. The same is true of the digital camera - once you learn to use the machines in Sam's Club or at WalMart, you can enlarge and crop your photographs and get them developed sometimes within minutes. I took about twenty photographs at the National Storytelling Festival in Jonesborough, Tennessee last week. There was no loading of film, no setting of f-stops, no changing of lenses - just a touch of a button to make something wide-angle or really close-up. After removing the memory card from the camera and inserting it into a machine at Sam's Club, spending about five minutes cropping out telephone wires or other extraneous stuff, I was told I could have them developed within twenty minutes, as they weren't busy right then.

The extremely tiny computer card in my camera, about the size of a postage stamp, holds two hundred images, whereas thirty-six were the most you could hope for with the old-fashioned roll of film. How many times have you taken photographs only to find that the film roll hadn't been inserted properly, and so none got recorded for posterity?

On my cell phone, I can have a different ring tone for thirty or forty of my closest friends, as if I could remember whose ring was "When the Saints Go Marching In" and whose was "Chopin's Polonaise." I can list friends or relatives so that I just have to punch one number on my cell phone for each of them. I can even get messages when my cell phone is turned off or left in the car, and it will identify the telephone number of the person calling when I turn it back on.

I'm often told that if I would just sit down at the computer and try doing all sorts of things, I'd learn faster. I think older people are afraid they're going to do something bad to the computer so they aren't as daring as younger people. A few days ago, I got out the cell phone manual and just tried punching all the keys and holding them down, since you get a different response when punching the same key or number for different periods of time. Well, I got to the last key, which is # and held it down. The message I got on the screen was that I had locked my cell phone, so that I couldn't call out on it or accept calls. To get it unlocked, I had to punch in my secret code, which I didn't have, since I'd never gotten one before. But, smart cell phone that it is, it gave me another message that said if I hadn't gotten a code yet, I could just punch in 4 zeros. I did and nothing happened. I then called Verizon, and they told me to punch in the last four numbers of my telephone number. I tried that - the last four numbers of my home number. When that didn't work, I called a friend, who figured out they meant the last four numbers of my cell phone number. Well, duh!

All the directions in the manual seem to be written by some foreign entity for which English is a second language or maybe even fourth. The words are usually grammatically correct, but some are obscure or inappropriate for the context.

The things that can be done with the computer are amazing and even more challenging. There are five members of the condo association board, and we can approve the minutes of the previous meeting over the Internet or look at the proposed budget or get as many as a dozen angry e-mails from residents about a dog tethered outside and barking early in the morning.

I can play Scrabble with three people consecutively, one in Tokyo, one in Australia, and one in Singapore in less than two hours. Or, I can set the computer to fifteen different levels of difficulty and play against it. It even has a name - *Maven*.

Sometimes, though, I long for the simpler life or think I might like to move to a small town somewhere, although someone reminded me that all these devices would just accompany me there. There are lots of advantages, too, of course. I can go to *Coupons4Indy* and print out coupons for my dry cleaners that let me have 30 per cent off cleaning and get my shirts done for thirty cents less than if I didn't have the coupon.

I thought retirement would mean I could stop and smell the flowers and not live at such a fast pace, but so far, it just means a smaller income.

A Trip to the State Fair

I've experienced loneliness a lot recently. It just seems to come upon me suddenly, with no warning. I've always liked to be in control of my own destiny, but I've learned that isn't always easy to do.

I still read a lot, listen to music more now - all kinds, from Dolly Parton to classical - have lunch with other groups of retirees, usually attend two of the three Scrabble groups that meet each week, play poker once a month, walk along the Monon Trail or the canal downtown, go to the swimming pool, see movies at theaters, as well as on DVD. It doesn't seem that I would have a whole lot of time to sit and mope or fret. Eight participants in the bereavement group, which formally lasted six weeks, agreed to meet monthly for lunch and discussion, so I'm not exactly alone a lot. I've also been doing some projects around the condo that I'd put off doing the last few years.

When my daughter said she was planning a visit for a week in August, I was pleased, especially since it overlapped with my son's vacation, and he would have my granddaughter, Savannah, all that week. Savannah is four, so we all decided to go to the Indiana State Fair on opening day. I'd forgotten all the sights at the Fair, as I hadn't been in several years. I'm not talking about the sideshows - just the view from the little shuttle train from the back entrance around to the front. If you have an outside seat, you can see some of the strangest sights.

It was perfect weather, sunny and then cloudy, but not too hot, low humidity, and no rain. We ate some of the usual - hot dogs, Italian sausage, gyros, cotton candy, milk shakes, fried Wisconsin cheese, elephant ears. While the others went around to look at the horses in one place - we'd just looked at the hogs and cows - I found a seat and looked through the program that listed all the photographs and who had submitted them and who had won, in preparation for a quick trip through the Family Arts Building. Another man sat down just a couple of chairs away and was eating about four of the abovementioned foods. He spotted a friend of his walking by, and they started talking about cholesterol levels and how they had given themselves the day off from thinking about cholesterol and calories and carbs. Then I heard one of them say that if he died today, it would take a week for them to wipe the smile off his face. I had to smile myself.

Of course, Savannah not only wanted to see the horses and the hogs but also the sheep and the roosters. She wanted to go on as many rides as she could, and now that she is so tall, she could go on many of them by herself, such as the small merry-go-round and Dodgem cars and motorcycles that went up and down and around. Her dad accompanied her on the larger carousel and the Ferris Wheel.

Since I didn't go on any of the rides, I was a sucker for the guy yelling at me as we walked by saying he could guess my weight (within three pounds) or my age (within two years.) Since I didn't want to have to get on the scales to prove a point, I said, "Okay, guess my age." he looked me over, up and down, and I noticed his looking at my children and grandchild, as well, and then wrote a number down on a piece of paper, putting it into his left hand. He then told me to tell him my age. I immediately thought he must have already had a bunch of small papers with different ages on them and would pull out the correct one, but I played along. When I told him I was sixty-nine, and he pulled out the paper that had fifty-seven written on it, I'll admit I felt pretty good.

When he told Savannah she could pick out any prize there, I knew for sure I'd been suckered into giving him $3 for something that at most cost about fifty cents to manufacture, as there were all these stuffed animals on display. There were a few larger prizes, though, off to the side, and Savannah chose one of the biggest - a pink balloon in the shape of a dolphin. When she squeezed one of the fins, it made a noise. She could have chosen any of the stuffed animals, but she has a ton of them already, and she loves pink. Needless to say, I ended up carrying that inflated pink porpoise the majority of the time we were there, which was a little bit awkward, but I could see the look on Charley's face that kept reminding me that I had gotten myself into that situation.

I got back at Charley, though, because when Savannah wanted to know if she could take it into the bathtub with her, I, being the grandfather, said, "Of course, that's where dolphins belonged - in the water." Savannah fell asleep on the shuttle train taking us back to the entrance near the parking lot, which meant Charley had to carry her several blocks through the campus of the School for the Deaf, where we had parked.

I'm glad I'm sixty-nine, though, and don't have to think about the Fair again for awhile, because Charley and Savannah are going back tomorrow with a group of friends, some of whom have small children, too. It may take a week before I wipe the smile off my face, just thinking about them.

The Road to Hell

The road to hell is paved with good intentions. This is a phrase I've heard said with a healthy dose of sarcasm over the years. Ever since hearing a beautiful variety of inspiring memoirs two weeks ago - some funny, some sad, but all beautifully written, I decided then and there that I'd really work on coming up with a great idea for a meaningful memoir for today's group. In fact, I thought, I'd start that same Wednesday night and so as not to put myself in a situation that required me to stay up half the night before finishing it or polishing up the sentence structure, or avoiding dangling participles, or looking in the Thesarus for another word that means the same as beautiful, which I've already used twice in the same paragraph.

But as good as my intentions were, somehow they got trampled upon by real life events or situations that seemed to cry out for priority handling - in fact, each yelling to me to "pick me first." I finally stopped procrastinating - no, not about writing a memoir - but about buying a new computer and hiring a computer consultant. He told me exactly what to buy and where I could get it cheapest, and that I should definitely get a DSL line, which would make my old 1997 computer obsolete. I couldn't find a word that meant obsolete to the nth degree. Computers are called old now if they are three or four years old and ancient if six or seven.

So I did all that and got the guy to come out and install it and tell me how to use it and instruct me about all the new computer icons on my desktop and the new language this computer uses. Bookmarks are no longer bookmarks - they're *favorites*. Now, of course, I've a new toy, I mean, a new machine that is going to make my life so much better, especially since I had to have a rough draft of a four-page newsletter for the Homeowners Association. I can also look at all the photographs my daughter sent of Hurricane Wilma and its aftermath in Cozumel and at all the photographs she is sending me of her travels to Russia and Norway. I've also got to send everyone in my address book my new e-mail address, for fear I'll miss some important information or an invitation to a pitch-in dinner. I'm also supposed to be studying up for the 3rd Annual Pacers' Foundation's Scrabble Tournament at Conseco Fieldhouse this Saturday, where I've learned at least sixty players are coming for the one-day event from all across Indiana and seven other neighboring states. I'm mainly doing this since gerontologists recommend keeping our minds alert and active. We're also supposed to continue with as many social activities as possible for fear of developing dementia and memory loss.

I also decided to use the free Pacers' ticket that comes as part of the Scrabble Tournament's registration fee to see my first Pacers' basketball game ever. The nearest I've gotten to watching a professional basketball game for many years was watching the old movie, *Hoosiers*, and recently having seen the newest basketball movie, based on a true account, called *Road to Glory*, recommended by Heartland Films. In fact, the latter movie was done so well that it was almost like a thriller.

Of course, I managed to see several other movies the past two weeks and a three-hour-long Golden Globe Awards show on TV.

My Christmas tree is still up, as I haven't had time to take it down and store all the ornaments away. I've spent a lot of time just wondering how long it was going to take me to get that task done, and if I could leave it up for another month or so.

All of the past two weeks hasn't been spent on just fun things or entertainment, though. I spent about six hours talking with seven or eight different people about getting two people I know into some counseling or therapy at their local mental health center. Since I've been retired for over nine years now, my contacts at mental health centers have all retired themselves or moved on, and I had to deal with people whose job seemed to be to put as many roadblocks in the paths of people trying to get help as possible in order to lighten their own caseloads.

I also went to a funeral home to try to lend a little support to a fellow Scrabble player whose identical twin brother had just died of cancer at age 38.

I had to find an appropriate birthday card for a memoir group member who's having a big birthday this week, when I could have been using that time to write a meaningful memoir that my children would cherish forever, or that might get a thoughtful "Hmm!" from this group or at least a knowing smile.

Somehow being a total failure in the memoir exercise this week, a disappointment to those who've come to expect something a *little* better, or just hoping for a laugh, I feel I've really let you down, but I didn't mean to. I promise to do better next time and won't bother you with any excuses next time, maybe, because, as the saying goes, "The road to hell is paved..."

Weight Watchers

Thoughts of wearing a bathing suit, heaven forbid skinny-dipping, worried me so much that three weeks ago I joined Weight Watchers. Of course, at the first weigh-in I weighed much more than I thought I did, because of having all my clothes on and my size twelve shoes. When I saw what I should weigh for my height (I've become shorter by about an inch and a half since I was eighteen) I thought I'd got there just in time.

The enthusiastic woman who took my registration materials and who gave the first lecture said she had lost 85 lbs. thirty-five years ago and kept the weight off all these years, so I thought there was hope.

There are now two plans you can use in Weight Watchers to help with shedding the weight - a point plan, where you can eat anything you want - there are no forbidden foods - but you have to keep track of how many points each food is, and you have a maximum number of points each day. I have twenty-six points, and then there are thirty-five "bonus points" that you can use anytime during the week - all on one day or five each day, however you want. The other plan allows you to eat any amounts of the acceptable foods, but you have to stick to their list. I decided to try the first plan and see what happens. The instructor said you could switch plans and try them both to see which fits you better.

I lost nine point four pounds the first week, and the instructor, someone new to me, as the other woman was on vacation, acted slightly ticked off. In fact, her entire lecture was about not trying to lose weight too fast and not being too stringent, and how men lost weight much more quickly at first than women, and how all women get bloated once a month and gain a little from water retention. I decided that I needed to lose at least another pound or two during the next week, as you're rewarded when you lose ten pounds.

The next week the first instructor was back and weighed me in. I had lost exactly six-tenths of a pound, so my total loss for the two weeks was ten pounds. If I had known it was going to be that close, I would have skipped breakfast or worn a pair of shoes that was lighter. Anyway, I got a red ribbon for my efforts and a round of applause. The third week I lost another two pounds, so I've lost a total of twelve pounds in the first three weeks.

It was interesting to see the others in the group. Most didn't seem very overweight. Most were women, but there were at least four other men there, one over 300 pounds. Once the women got started talking about recipes and how to prepare cauliflower to make it seem like mashed potatoes, I began to lose interest.

I did find out that Applebee's offers an entire menu of items with the Weight Watchers points printed beside them. Twice now I've had grilled shrimp and steak, brown rice, and broccoli and used up only seven points of my daily twenty-six. Of course, you can eat as much broccoli as you want, as it doesn't count anything, not even one point. I've learned to eat the stalks and all. Applebee's even has desserts for three to five points. I've become a real Applebee's fan.

There's a website called "Dotti's Restaurants A to Z" which lists most of the popular chain restaurants nationwide and prints their menus with the Weight Watchers number of points beside each menu item. You don't want to visit Bob Evans or Cheeseburger Heaven, but there are a lot of places that prepare nutritional food with not many calories. You can eat almost all the fruits and vegetables you want if you don't put sugar or sauces on them.

I don't know if I'll be able to get down to my goal weight, as that means I have to lose thirty-nine pounds. I think I'll give it a try, though. I just went through some old papers and things I'd had stored away and found my old draft registration card. My weight was listed at 148 pounds at age eighteen. I've certainly gained a lot out of life, if you want to look at it that way.

I like the way the instructor ends each class - "Hope to see less of you next week."

A Life Almost Totaled

I had just had dinner at the MCL Cafeteria in Castleton and was waiting at the stoplight. The light turned green and I proceeded across. I had gotten about three lanes across the intersection when there was a loud bang on the passenger side of the car and my car was swirling around - in fact, the steering wheel seemed to have a mind of its own. I just went with the flow, it seems. The car turned completely around and left me facing the opposite direction in the entrance lane to the parking lot across the intersection. I literally was almost in shock. I saw a car with its driver's door open and a man rushing to my car, saying, "It's my fault, I went through a red light." The first thing that struck my mind is, one's never supposed to say that after an accident, according to all the instructions from the insurance companies. But, it certainly was his fault, and I told him so. He asked if I was all right, and I had to tell him to wait a minute, that I didn't know. I had a little pain, but it seemed as though it was due to the seat belt's tightening.

Of course, by this time several people had gathered around the car, all asking me if I was all right and when I mentioned my sore chest, they seemed to be thinking that maybe I'd had a heart attack or that I had hit the steering wheel, neither of which was true. Two people said they had already called 911, and since it was around 8 PM, dark, and drizzling rain, I just decided to stay in the car. A woman with a child came up and said that she was right behind me at the stoplight, that she had seen the whole thing, and that the man had run a red light. She stayed the entire forty minutes until the police came, as she said people often say one thing but then change their story later. Another woman came up and said she saw the same thing, but from across the street. Both women gave me their names and telephone numbers.

I called my son, who was at work, and asked if he could call a neighbor to come and pick me up, which he did, after I assured him I wasn't hurt. No one else had been hurt, either, even though the guy who crashed into me had his wife and mother-in-law in the car with him.

Dealing with the guy's insurance company, especially the claims adjuster, proved very difficult. My car, paid for and kept so well for five years, was totaled. At least my life wasn't.

Loneliness

I never thought I'd be lonely. I guess that means I had a distorted view of the universe. Not only am I lonely, six months after Ann has died, but I'm lonesome and I'm alone a lot. I could be with others, I suppose. I skipped Scrabble Club tonight and went to a movie by myself. I've always liked to go to the movies - since I was very young. I like comedies, dramas, melodramas, westerns, action films, foreign films, documentaries - almost all kinds except those with cartoon characters or animation of any sort.

When I was growing up, one could attend a movie on Saturdays at a second-run theater for only nine cents. I distinctly remember because I can recall when they raised the price to a dime. Not only did you see a fairly new movie - one that had already played downtown, though - you also saw perhaps The March of Time, a newsreel, previews of coming attractions, a B-movie, and a cartoon or two. I didn't mind the short cartoons they showed, but they were just something mainly for the kids, I thought. Through the years Ann and I often saw a movie a week. We liked going out to a theater rather than watching a video, although, of course, we did that, too, after our son bought us a VCR when he got his first decent-paying job.

I like to watch all the credits at the end of the movie - something that is very rare in Indiana; most people are up and out of their seats the minute they start rolling, or else they stand up and talk and block your view of the screen.

Next week is the last meeting of the bereavement group. I'm ambivalent about it. It hasn't seemed to help that much; three people dropped out of the group during the first three meetings, but that still left nine participants, as well as the two facilitators. They tried very hard to be facilitators and not therapists. They never gave advice or made any judgmental remarks, unless they were of the kind that said you were perhaps being too hard on yourself, or that perhaps it would be better, if you hesitated or were uncomfortable, to wait until later in the group to talk. At the next meeting, which is also the last formal meeting with the facilitators and at the same location, we are supposed to decide if we would like to continue as a group or just meet occasionally or meet for lunch or something of that sort. They said that someone should be prepared to propose the continuation of the group or that it could just end. I really don't know how I will vote, if it comes down to a vote. I suppose I wouldn't mind meeting for lunch once a month but actually I already have enough groups or people who want to meet for lunch or dinner. I could always call some friends or a couple I know for that kind of occasion. The difficult thing is asking someone - just one person - to go out to lunch or dinner or to a movie or a concert or a walk. I certainly don't want to start "dating" but how is this supposed to be handled by a widower? I've gone over a list of possible people to ask and can find reasons for not asking any of them. When you're pushing seventy, it seems more difficult to ask someone out to coffee or dinner or a movie that it ever did at sixteen or eighteen or twenty-two.

Perhaps you don't think I have a dilemma. I halfway approached this topic the other day with a group of people who had gathered early at one of the Scrabble Clubs by starting off the conversation saying I had found the next woman for me - they knew I was kidding but they acted shocked anyway until I told them it was Teresa Heinz Kerry, and then they seemed to breathe a sigh of relief. Several said there was a group of people who got together by answering a personal ad in *Nuvo* - a group of strangers, essentially, who just went to the movies together. I can't envisage myself going with a bunch of people I don't know to a movie - perhaps on a hike, such as with the Indianapolis Hiking Club, but not a movie.

I had another friend (male) who said there were Websites one could go to on the Internet where you typed in a rather detailed history of your traits and demographics and then you could also list the requirements or traits you'd like in another person. Somehow this entire conversation seemed almost surreal. The other guy, who is in his 50's, divorced, with two grown children, told me of some of the disasters he's had by doing this or answering personal ads in the newspapers. All of the people he met turned out to be just about the worst horror stories you could imagine, and yet he was still involved in it. I figured that if I couldn't find someone on my own, I deserved to be alone for the rest of my life.

I read several books on being a widower and how everyone was different and how there was no set time to start going out again. Some said a year, some said six months, or even three months; some said two years. Some, like a few of my acquaintances, said it doesn't matter what other people think, and I certainly feel that way. I can honestly say I don't care what anyone thinks of my behavior in this regard. I feel it's a very personal matter, and, in fact, it's something that Ann tried to discuss with me; but I always refused to enter into a discussion of it because it was ridiculous. I couldn't imagine myself being in a situation like that anyway, even though we both knew that she was almost certain to precede me in death.

I guess I'll go on like this until something changes. I've always liked to be in control of my own destiny, but I've certainly learned that that isn't always the case. When the weather is nice I like to walk along the canal downtown or go to lunch and to some fun activity with my son and granddaughter every two weeks. I wouldn't say I'm lucky exactly, but I guess this will have to do for now.

At the Edge of the Ocean

I probably made the last trip I will make to Florida, certainly the last one I'll ever drive, especially by myself. I may decide at some future time to fly down if I can get a direct flight to wherever it is I'm going.

I drove to New Smyrna Beach, Florida, the last week in June - an 1,100 mile trip one way from door to door where my twin sisters have a family reunion every year for two weeks during the summer. New Smyrna Beach is my brother-in-law Roy's hometown, so that's why this small town about twenty miles south of Daytona Beach was chosen. I think they've been going for thirty-four years. This was only the second time I'd been.

The beach there, the ocean, the palm trees, the sand, the skies, the weather all seem timeless and ageless. The Spanish moss growing on the live oak trees, the seagulls, the heron, the ibis, the sandpipers, the shells (or lack of them) all seem the same.

The one view in Florida that hasn't changed one iota during my entire lifetime is looking out to sea - at the sky, the ocean, the waves, the horizon - from about twenty feet from the water's edge. It looks *exactly* the same as it did as far back as I can remember, which is when I was about five years old. Even the shades of the water haven't changed - going from a sandy-colored ocean to light greenish to dark greenish, then almost black all the way to the horizon. The occasional shrimp boat or freighter is so far away that it also looks just like it did sixty-five to seventy years ago.

Turning around 180 degrees, facing the shore, the view has changed about 90 per cent - all new homes and condos. The beach is even different - the sea wall is either low or buried, and now there are small sand dunes everywhere. It's the contrast between the two views that is so interesting. In fact, there's something that makes one prone to philosophize just staring at the sea and its surroundings - something about the salt air that seems elemental and primordial, if you will. Looking again toward the shore, one can see that there are still a few old cottages, from the 1930's and 40's, but many more new *cottages* - three-story houses or multiple-apartment houses and lots of condominiums, especially the high-rise kind. The last have all kinds of rules and regulations, usually a gate to keep people from entering the enclosed pool areas and courtyards filled with oleander bushes, hibiscus, and bougainvillea. Most use a code that you have to punch in to get through the gates, and the fences are too high for interlopers to climb over, although not all of them.

Thundershowers crop up almost every afternoon in the summer months, but they are mostly scattered, coming suddenly and without much warning, but not lasting long. They tend to cool the temperature a little, too. People scurry to gather their belongings - beach bags, coolers, tents, beach chairs, and umbrellas, because often the winds are quite strong. What had been a huge crowd around the pool, in the ocean, and scattered all over the beach will leave the beach deserted and lonely in just a few minutes. People evacuate quickly so as not to get struck by lightning. The sun may reappear several times a day between the storms.

Inside, the children and teenagers are usually restless and unwilling to think their time on the beach or at the pool has ended for the day. TVs are turned on, snacks are devoured, while the older people may head for a nap. A few retreat only to their balconies, which all face the ocean. Some bring out the cards or board games. Plans for dinner are discussed, with many opting for a seafood restaurant. I played spades one evening and poker another with three adults and three teenaged boys (my great nephews.) They got very rowdy and loud and won almost every hand at poker, even though they didn't know how to shuffle or handle the cards well and usually dealt some of them face-up by mistake. They accused one of my sisters, their grandmother, of being a poor loser, when really just luck was on their side.

The good news is that with even eating lots of food, I did manage quite a few long walks along the beach, so that when I returned from my trip, I'd actually lost a pound.

I've been lucky enough to have seen the ocean every year of my life, if not in Florida, then in Georgia, South or North Carolina, New Jersey, Massachusetts, or Mexico, so who knows if I'll return next year to view the ocean's edge once again - not if I have to drive.

Even Dreams Have Expiration Dates

I got this title from something I was reading not long ago, but I can't remember where or who wrote it. I liked it, though. You know I have to have a title to work by - it's what I start out with, rather than write something and then later think about what I should call it.

I'm going to a fairly small high school reunion Christmas luncheon in Jacksonville, Florida on Friday, flying down on Thursday. I started wondering what people did with their lives; I'm sure most are retired now, since everyone is approximately the same age - seventy or seventy-one. Did people become what they wanted? Did they change their minds or settle for less? A few people I've heard about seemed quite successful, and they aren't the ones I would have particularly thought of - a judge, a plastic surgeon, an architect, and others in various businesses that have done quite well.

Almost all have been married, although many have been divorced or widowed; only a very few never married at all. Some are deceased, of course. There were some real surprises - one painfully shy girl who never volunteered to answer a teacher's question and looked as if she might pass out when the teacher called on her - had become a successful real estate broker, living in Florida half the year and California the other half. She had been the first woman president of the Riverside Lions Club and recently presided over their 50th Anniversary Celebration.

I got this information from a book that was put together at the time of the 50th high school reunion, which was quite a big affair, spread out over an entire weekend.

I've mentioned a few of my unfulfilled dreams before - such as always having wanted to learn to play the piano, write a book, or get something (not technical or related to psychology) published. I've decided that the first two had expiration dates that have already passed. I think I'll still keep the last one though and see if I can make it happen sometime during 2008. I think I'll put December, 2008 as the expiration date - that gives me a little time, but sets a deadline, too.

Storytelling

Jonesborough, the oldest town in the state of Tennessee, is the site of the National Storytelling Festival. Its population is around 8,000, but about 12,000 more people descend upon this quaint little town the first weekend in October. I'd been to hear several storytellers here in Indianapolis at the Indiana History Center, so I was eagerly looking forward to two and a half days crowded with storytellers in six big white tents that each held 2,000 people. The festival ran from 10 AM to 10 PM, except for Saturday night when there was a special Cabaret performance from 10 PM to midnight.

Although I'd made reservations in February, most of the near-by motels were full; I was lucky to get a room in a motel in Johnson City, Tennessee, which is about fifteen minutes away. While Doris and I were there, we came upon a large bed-and-breakfast right downtown, but any thoughts of getting a room there for next year were quickly squelched by the sign on its front door that said it was sold out already for 2007. We could see why because most of us parked at the local high school parking lot and then took a shuttle bus into town for a dollar each way. We found we could park on people's private property right on the edge of town for $10 a day, so after the first day, that's what we did.

The town had cobblestone streets and sidewalks and was decorated with Fall displays of pumpkins and mums. There were no chain restaurants at all in the downtown section - only small restaurants and antique shops. In addition, there were the National Storytelling Building, a modern library, a Visitors' Center, and a church in almost every block. Most of the churches served lunches of soup, chili, sandwiches, and freshly baked goods for only six dollars a person. There were long tables, where you sat with others that you may not know, but everyone was very friendly. We had an interesting person come and sit with us, even though there was plenty of room elsewhere. The woman's name was Echo, which was on a large card that was hung around her neck, and she was a librarian. During the next couple of days, we passed her on the streets many times or saw her at the Storytelling Center, or bumped into her in the ice cream store. Truly, her name was an omen. There were several outdoor stands with hot coffee, soft drinks, or hot cocoa. There was also a line of tents arranged like a food court, with pizza and all sorts of delicious State Fair food but not for those trying to eat healthily. Although you could order beer or wine in many of the little restaurants, we saw only one guy order a beer for lunch one day. He asked the waitress to recommend a beer and she said, "I don't know, I've been pregnant or breast-feeding ever since I've worked here." There was no rowdiness or loudness and people seemed genuinely friendly - many resembling what I imagine the hippies of the 1960's and 1970's would look like if they had survived until today. They were mostly adults; very few children attended. We had a nice dinner one night with friends from college days, one who had come all the way from Virginia Beach, Virginia and another from Florence, South Carolina. In fact, this was their eighth time attending.

After one performance, Doris left her cushion in one of the tents; when we realized it, she went back and there it was, just waiting for her - no one had bothered it, even though the tent was filling up for the next performance.

I had heard several of the presenters, but I had especially liked Carmen Agra Deedy, so we tried to attend all of her presentations during the three-day period. At every one of her performances, the tents were full and over a hundred people were willing to stand up all around the edges of the tents and in back. The sound was great and the chairs not bad if you had been warned, as we had, to bring along a stadium seat to put in them.

Carmen escaped from Cuba with her family when she was four, and the family was relocated to Decatur, Georgia, where she grew up. She can speak Spanish perfectly, as well as affect a Southern drawl that seems the genuine thing. She also can sound quite sophisticated, with no trace of either accent, when she wants, which is usually not when telling a story.

She told of being left at the public library one Saturday by her older sister, who told her to go in and stay there until she came back for her. She was about seven and had never been in a library before, and after having a conversation with the head librarian, was ushered into the children's room that was lined with books for children of all ages. When she said that she didn't have any idea what book to choose, the librarian told her that she should just look around and that ... " the book would choose her." After marveling at so many books, Carmen saw one book that was slightly sticking out of the shelf; she took it down and started reading it - it was by an author named E.B. White. She was engrossed in reading it when she heard her sister return to pick her up, so she brought the book out for the librarian to check out. She was told that the book was for older children and that she should pick out another one. After a rather heated exchange, she blurted out that she had to have this book - that "...it had chosen her." She ended up being fascinated with the book and got into trouble trying to read under the covers each night with a flashlight - the story of a spider who dies at the end of the book.

We were intrigued for three days and laughed hard for about twelve hours a day. As cold as it was in the evening, the stories and the camaraderie certainly warmed us up.

Musings
(Or Maybe Just a Better-Sounding Name for Scattered Thoughts)

I've been trying to engage in some different and interesting activities recently, to broaden my perspective. By the way, that's not too easy at this age. Changes are often accompanied by anxiety or befuddlement. I can't remember who said, "A mind once stretched by new thoughts can never regain its original shape."

I went to a lecture and slide show on Sunday by artist Marilyn Price, an old Unitarian dinner-discussion group friend who had been to Machu Picchu in the Peruvian Andes and kept a journal, as she has always done for the last 40 years or so. But, her journal starts with a sketch, in ink, no less, or maybe with as many as four small sketches a day. She then goes back and fills in the spaces that she leaves between the drawings with notes about that day, and these notes are written each night and in calligraphy. Machu Picchu is the ancient Inca city whose terraced stonework is linked by 3,000 steps. There are no good explanations about how the massive stones were placed in such regular formations, a group of which was placed as a way to keep time. One theory, which sounds as plausible as any of the others, is that it was built and settled by inhabitants from outer space. There is evidence that the people who lived there perished very suddenly, too.

Marilyn was asked what the cuisine was, since she had remarked that the food was delicious. She gave one example - roasted guinea pig. She said they knew the meat was fresh because there were all these guinea pigs running around in the kitchen of the family where she and Don had been invited for a meal. She said it tasted a little like rabbit.

I got two very contrasting e-mails this morning from my son, Charley, and daughter, Elizabeth. Charley said that he may not have time to talk to me, as he usually does on Mondays, his day off work, as he had plans to take the dog in for a rabies shot and heartworm test and medication, at a probable cost of $170, and then he had to take his bicycle in for a tune-up so that he could start exercising on it as soon as the weather became a little more inviting. The bike repairs were likely to cost around $125, and he seemed concerned about these extra costs. Now Charley had been relatively thin his entire life (until age 41) but stopped smoking two years ago and now is gaining weight and beginning to turn into his father, which he no doubt wants to try to modify with exercise as best he can.

My daughter's e-mail indicated that her life was a little more adventuresome. She just finished one contract on a Princess Cruise Line ship and went to Cozumel, Mexico, where she lives when she is not working, which is usually three months of the year. She flew last week, all expenses paid, to New York's diamond district, where she learned all about the gems she will be selling on her upcoming stint on a Princess Cruise in the Baltic, that will go from Copenhagen to St. Petersburg every ten days. Now back in Cozumel, she will board another ship in a week or so and go on a three-week cruise. The itinerary she sent me: Flies to Bangkok on March 26th, then to Singapore, next to Da Nang, Vietnam, Hong Kong, Shanghai, Nagasaki, Pusan, Korea, Xingang and Dalian, China, and then Shanghai again, with days at sea interspersed with each port. She then flies back to Cozumel where she will stay a couple of weeks until she joins another ship to sail to the Baltic. And I'm just hoping for another trip to New Smyrna Beach, Florida and one to Brown County before I get too old to drive.

Last week I also played in a Scrabble Tournament, went to hear a storyteller, saw a funk music art exhibit, and then a jazz and blues concert, all at the Indiana History Center, had lunch with Barbara at a new little cafe near where I live called the A 2 Z Cafe. The owner is Egyptian and his wife is Mexican, and it was a neat little place with a somewhat different menu. (Nothing even approaching guinea pig, however.)

I ran across this quotation in an old Scrabble Newsletter from a club director who was retiring and moving away. It was in my desk in a folder labeled "Miscellaneous," which I often go through trying to find a topic interesting enough on which to write a memoir. The saying, to which no author is attributed, goes: "As you journey through life, choose your destinations well, but do not hurry there. You will arrive soon enough. Wander back roads and forgotten paths, keeping your destination like the fixed point of a compass. Seek out new voices, strange sights, and ideas foreign to your own. Such things are riches for the soul. And if, upon arrival, you find that your destination is not exactly as you had dreamed, do not be disappointed. Think of all you would have missed but for the journey there, and know that the true worth of your travels lies not in where you come to be at the journey's end, but in who you come to be along the way."

I may not even recognize myself by the beginning of next year.

Household Drudgery

I was going to call this *Household Chores*, but I looked up the word *chore* and found it means light tasks around the house or farm. I needed a stronger word. I've learned to do a lot of chores in the past year or so that I had just never done before, certainly not on a regular basis. You'd think that some things are almost self-explanatory, but they're not. Loading the dishwasher - now you have to learn to do that. Things have to be placed a certain way if they're not to be broken or if they're to get clean. The glasses go upside down, for some reason. And then there are those little magnets - to tell you when the contents are dirty or clean that I always forget to change. Once you learn, though, there's really not much to it. Cleaning floors, now, is a little more difficult. You literally have to get down on your hands and knees to clean the scuff marks off the floor before you mop it. You have to learn what cleaning agents to use so that you don't damage the surface. I can never get it to glisten - like in the ads. Those aqua blue things you put in the back of the johns don't really work. They just color the water bluish, so that you can't see the dirt as easily.

At one point, when we were having to drive back and forth to the hospital almost every single day for weeks in a row, we didn't seem to find time to do any cleaning beyond the dishes and the clothes and emptying the trash baskets, etc., so I decided to call a cleaning service. I looked in the yellow pages and saw the name of one company that I'd heard about where maids come in and size the place up and see if there is anything worth stealing. Then they have their friend break in and take all the things worth anything. So I thought I'd better ask some neighbors who had cleaning ladies. I did but their cleaning ladies were all booked up and not taking any new customers.

I finally called a cleaning agency, part of a national chain, but locally owned. They would send two people who worked together and the charge would be thirty-five dollars an hour. I told the woman that we really just wanted the bathrooms and the kitchen cleaned, especially the floors, and maybe the entrance hall floor. She said that sounded like a two-hour job. These are the only areas in our house that aren't carpeted, and I did know how to vacuum the carpet (although there is another entire story there.) So, shortly after the prearranged time, two people, a man and a woman, showed up. They appeared to be Mexican, but they may have been from another Latino country. They also appeared to be a mother and her son, but again they may have just been a middle-aged woman and a younger man. She obviously was in charge and told him what to do. She did all this in Spanish. I showed them around and told them essentially what I had told the owner of the company, and the woman made some noises, which I took to be sounds meaning she understood what I was saying and to be agreeing. I then asked if they had any questions and when they indicated no, I told her that Ann was lying down in the master bedroom and that I would be in the study upstairs, if they needed anything. I warned them about not leaving the front door open because of our two cats. They then went to their car and lugged in a huge bunch of cleaning materials, mops, buckets, brooms, brushes, vacuum cleaner, paper towels, rags, etc. I left them to go about their business, which they did with gusto. The guy started cleaning the Venetian blinds in the kitchen and the woman started scrubbing the sink. The next time I looked in on them, the guy was dusting the entry hall and the woman was on her hands and knees scrubbing at scuff marks on the kitchen floor.

About an hour and twenty minutes later, I heard the door open a couple of times and then nothing - total silence. I looked around and saw neither cleaning person. I opened the front door and went to the driveway, where I saw them driving off about as fast as they worked. I went back into the kitchen, thinking they may have left a bill or a note or something, but nothing. I remarked to Ann that things looked pretty good and about how fast they had worked. I noticed that it seemed awfully warm in the house. I also noticed that the kitchen clock has stopped working. It didn't take long to figure out that they had dusted it and one of the hands had become detached. I tried to fix it, but to no avail. I then noticed that it was getting really warm. I checked the thermostat and found it set on 85 degrees instead of the usual 70 degrees at which we keep it. I surmised that the guy had done something to the clock and the thermostat when he was dusting. The thermostat seemed okay, and the house began cooling down. I called the cleaning company, got their answering machine, and said that the cleaners had really done a good job, but mentioned both the clock and the thermostat. In the meantime, our son came over, and he looked at the clock and was able to fix it, so I called the cleaning company back and left a message about that, too. I finally got a message on our answering machine one day from the owner, just wanting to check and see if everything was all right now. I called her back and while I had her on the line, I asked if either of the cleaners spoke any English. She said the guy didn't, but that the woman understood some. Well, time passed and things got dirty again, as everything around the house has a tendency to do, so this time I called and asked about rescheduling the cleaners, and asked the owner if she would talk to them about not dusting the thermostat or the clock. She said she would.

The next time they were scheduled, I let them in and demonstrated about not cleaning the clock or touching the thermostat, and they both nodded their heads and smiled. Still not a word of English or at least any that I could understand.

Once a week now I sit down with the newspapers and clip the coupons and read Heloise. Did you know that baking soda and vinegar will clean all the drains? At least the way it bubbles up, I figure it's got to be doing something. Now mind you, these things wouldn't be so difficult to do, but I've got to do them in addition to all my usual chores, such as changing the furnace filter, getting the oil changed in the cars, doing the grocery shopping, preparing all the food, paying the bills, and the biggest chore of all - waiting in waiting rooms - at the doctor's, the hospital, for the chemo, for the CAT Scans, for the chest X-rays, and at the pharmacist's. At least others are aware of all this, and that's why they call them waiting rooms, but that's a whole other story, too.

What If or Whatever?

I had a bad week last week. Almost nothing seemed to go well or on schedule or as I had expected. Maybe it's the last part of that sentence that had me caught up in turmoil. I decided that I needed to get the master bedroom repainted and the attached bath re-wallpapered. I'd also had a leak in the ceiling of the dining area downstairs and thought I might as well get that repaired by the handyman and then get the same painters who were doing the bedroom to add the ceiling in the dining room to their painting list.

Now you might wonder why I didn't do my own painting and even wallpapering. I had, as a matter of fact, done most of the interior painting in previous years, but I hadn't really wallpapered anything since Ann and I did the entrance hall in our other house about twenty years ago and woke up the next morning to find hundreds of small bubbles in the thick vinyl wallpaper. A call to an expert convinced us to invest in the largest hyperdermic needle we could find without encountering really strange looks from the pharmacist at the nearby drugstore. We meticulously went around and burst each and every bubble by injecting a little wallpaper glue with the needle and lo and behold, it worked and the wallpaper dried evenly, and you couldn't even tell where the little bubbles had been the next day.

Well, the main reason I didn't want to do my own painting is that the bedroom has a cathedral ceiling, and there was no way I could reach it or the top part of the walls on two sides, and besides I didn't want to fall off a ladder at my age. Who would take care of me? Who'd even find me, if I hit my head or something? No, I thought I should be cautious and get the work done by professionals. A clerk at the Castleton Sherwin-Williams store said she'd recommend several good painters, especially one whom she described as a Christian painter who was okay to leave in the house alone if I needed to leave while he was there. Just don't call him on a Sunday, she said. So, I did contact him; he came out and gave me an estimate, which seemed reasonable, so I asked if he could do it anytime soon, and we set a day for last Tuesday. I took down the curtains, emptied the walk-in closet of absolutely everything, as he was going to paint the shelves in there, too, and moved the lamps and other objects out of the room - into the only other room upstairs, the guest bedroom. Of course, when he arrived at 10 minutes before the scheduled 8 a.m. appointment, I was ready, if not yet fully functioning.

He had brought two helpers with him, and they soon had taken down the curtain rods, all the blinds, and moved most of the furniture out into the loft. He unplugged everything, even the cable TV, but I asked him not to unplug the telephone or answering machine, and he begrudgingly agreed. At about 11: 30, he said they were going to stop for a half-hour to get lunch but would be back to put on the second coat of paint after that. I then went up and looked and was pleased with the way it looked. They came back in less than half an hour and started repainting. Then one guy came down to do the dining room ceiling and was soon finished. They cleaned up, asked where the vacuum cleaner was, moved all the furniture back in and arranged it, for the most part, as it had been. Of course, later I found that the two night stands had been reversed, so I had to empty their contents, which was easier than moving them. That night I noticed that the TV didn't work. I checked the plugs and they seemed secure, except I had to move a huge chest of drawers about a foot away from the wall to check. I knew what the problem was right away, though. They had plugged a lamp into one socket and the TV into the bottom socket, which is controlled by a wall switch, and that's why I was using a multiple power strip to put them all on the circuit not controlled by the light switch. Of course, the TV had to be reprogrammed, but it did most of it automatically, even though it's an old set..

The next day I noticed that a big spot showed up where about half the leak was and looked even worse than it had before because the ceiling looked so glaringly white in contrast. I called and he said they'd come back before their first job on Monday and re-seal with some Wizard sealer and repaint it and it shouldn't take long at all, but would a little before 8 a.m. on Monday be okay? Of course, I said yes.

After waiting for the wallpaperer to come on Saturday afternoon, I finally called him, and not being able to reach him, left a message. He called a little later and said he was running late and would be out in a couple of hours to give me the estimate. A couple more hours passed, so I went to get the mail. Of course, he called back while I was gone, and the message said he still had an hour of cleaning up to do and that I could call and re-schedule or he'd understand if I didn't and to have a nice day. Yeah, right. I finally got him to come out and he gave me an estimate, which didn't seem too expensive, but he said he only had one day, Friday, April 7th, free until after mid-May. I told him that the wallpaper was going to take four or five days to arrive, so it wouldn't be in until Thursday or Friday. He said not to worry, if I was told four or five days, it would be in in four, so that's where I stand with that - a little anxious, but optimistic.

I set out about six-thirty last Friday to pick out the wallpaper. I hadn't been in the store more than a few minutes when the skies starting pouring heavy rain, the lights flickered several times, and the sirens went off. It wasn't very conducive to picking out wallpaper - that not only had to match the new paint colors but also the color of the bathroom tiles, as well. After determining that I needed eight double rolls, the clerk told me that was only if I got a pattern that repeated itself often. I finally chose a pattern that repeated itself, ordered the rolls, which were in stock in the warehouse, but would take another week to arrive, and then even with my 15 per cent discount, almost emptied my bank account.

As I was leaving Sherwin-Williams, the sun actually came out as the TV was announcing that a tornado had touched down in Brownsburg. I headed over to the MCL in Castleton and thought that would be as safe a place as any in a big storm or if another tornado came.

Next I went to Penney's where I thought it would be easy to order two wooden blinds for the stairwell's two windows - one short but extra wide and one narrow but extra long. Trying to measure with a measuring tape from the stairs, as I couldn't get a ladder on the stairs, was an adventure in itself. The salesclerk said I had three days to double-check the measurements, because they had to be exact for the made-to-order blinds. The wooden blinds were $230 each but with the big sale price and my 20 per cent coupon off above and beyond that, they would only cost $79 each - a real bargain, I thought, until I read the fine print about the no-return policy on specially-ordered blinds and had to sign a paper stating such.

Maybe I'll survive the next few weeks - or maybe I won't - whatever.

What's Important and What's Not

Each morning I get up, wash my face, comb my hair, brush my teeth with a battery-operated toothbrush - a great invention - take two pills, and go downstairs. I fix a bowl of cereal, pour a glass of orange juice, open the garage door to get the newspaper, and sit at the kitchen table, eating breakfast and reading the *Indianapolis Star*. Are any of these details important? I don't know. I've been browsing through books on writing, and a lot of them say that the truth is in the details. They also say to sit down and write, every day, even if only for a few minutes. Of course I just read somewhere that "...trying to speak about reality is like trying to send a kiss by a messenger."

Many of the books say to reveal yourself in your writings. I think my morning routine reveals a lot about me, but is it interesting? Does my writing have to be interesting to anyone else, or even to me? Many authors say that you must just write - for yourself, or the truth, or because you have to and you should not write for any audience. Writing for an audience is something that should be done only in instructions for assembling something or telling how to use some appliance or used only in technical articles, such as scientific writing and research, so that someone could exactly replicate your study if he/she wanted to do such a thing.

I'm always reading something - I usually have at least two books going at the same time, several magazines, and weekly newspapers or journals. Are there books which changed my life? I think so, but how would I know? I think my life looks pretty linear - it doesn't look like a Wall Street chart of the stock market. But who's to say I wouldn't have made a jump in another direction or taken off down a different road all of a sudden if I had read a particular book?

What are some of the candidates for books that changed my life - or not, as the case may be? Well, I liked *The Fountainhead* and *Atlas Shrugged*, both by Ayn Rand. I think the thing I liked about them was the rugged individuality of her characters. I was shocked when I read *Johnny Got His Gun* by Dalton Trumbo, because I didn't think there could be another book as antiwar, except for Mark Twain's *The War Prayer*. I thought I learned some things about prejudice and bigotry in unlikely little books like *My Sweet Charlie*. Kurt Vonnegut's semi-autobiographical novels and Anne Lamott's books, especially *Plan B,* said a great deal about creativity and about religion or the lack of it. Anne Tyler' books revealed a lot about family interactions. I learned a lot of things about the universe and its origins in *Just Six Numbers* by Martin Rees and *A Brief History of Time* by Stephen Hawking, and a lot about dying with as much dignity as possible in *Let Me Die Before I Wake* by Derek Humphrey

Johnny Got His Gun is about an American soldier missing in action and hideously injured in World War I. He can't do anything but endure his tomb-like existence. It was published in 1939 and meant to be a pacifist statement at the beginning of World War II. It was reissued in paperback during the Vietnam War. It could just as easily apply to soldiers maimed in Iraq today. The main character is a veteran who can't communicate because he has no jaws, no eyes, no mouth, and discovers this gradually, as he regains consciousness. He can't be dead because he's curious. He wonders how much you can lose of yourself and still not be dead. He starts to become panicky, but he then becomes calm as he surveys his situation. He thinks, "What a hell of a dream!" But it wasn't a dream. It's a fascinating book that would make a pacifist out of anyone who read it. The thing is, you probably wouldn't read the book unless you were already a pacifist.

A Non-Stop Flight

I left Indianapolis Airport on Thursday, December 8th at 1:35 PM, and my son later told me that at about 2:15 PM snow started coming down at the rate of about an inch an hour until there were 7.7 inches of snow on the ground. I had barely escaped. I went to Jacksonville, Florida, which is situated in the very northeastern corner of Florida, just eighteen miles from the coast. It's only thirty-five miles from Georgia but 365 miles from Miami, so it's not quite as tropical as the other cities in Florida that most tourists visit.

The occasion for my going there was to visit my sister and brother-in-law, who had just retired and moved into a new home. They had been threatening to visit me if I didn't visit them, so I chose the lesser of the two evils. I've always been one to adhere strictly to the old adage that guests and fish smell after three days, but since I only wanted to fly on a non-stop flight, the first reservation I could get back to Indianapolis was early Tuesday morning, so I was there almost five full days. My sister made sure she had scheduled things for about eighteen hours each day.

I actually had been looking forward to going for a visit and planned it to coincide with my high school's 52nd Christmas Reunion Luncheon. Now the big reunions have been planned every five years, but there's a small group of people who meet the first Monday of each month at a Piccadilly Cafeteria, and they always plan a larger event for the Christmas season at a restaurant instead of the cafeteria. Many more former graduates show up for the December luncheon, and most are from the Jacksonville area, including all the little nearby towns, such as Orange Park and Mandarin or the beaches. I decided to go and had already talked to one of the women who was involved in the planning of all these events. She told me who had already made reservations and they included many people I knew, some of whom I hadn't seen since 1953 and some I hadn't seen since the last reunion I had attended in 1978. Since two girls I had dated had made reservations, I thought it would be interesting. One woman, LeAnne, was the only woman still working; she was a dean at the local university, having sold her insurance company eight years ago. She still looked attractive. She said she'd been divorced three times.

The other woman, Kathleen, who had made reservations but had not shown up, had had triple bypass surgery the day of the reunion, I later learned from her son.

There were about fifty at the luncheon, about forty of whom were actual former students whom I knew or remembered. Most looked liked older versions of what they had looked like, some much older. Only one person looked much younger; in fact, I would have said like someone in her middle forties, instead of the 70- and 71-year-olds that we all were. Ann Manry Kenyon had been a cheerleader, and she had married a football player, but he had passed away last year. She's an internationally known artist, primarily a portrait painter, who commands a great deal of money for each painting. She just recently painted the First Lady of Florida's portrait and had it unveiled at a ceremony in Washington, D.C. I wouldn't swear that she hadn't had a little surgical help in staying young, but her looks were of someone much younger.

She wasn't the only one who had been quite successful; in fact, I wondered if it's only the successful who attend such functions. A good friend of mine sold his business when he was around age fifty and had retired at that age. He had remained active, especially in his church, which, of course, I asked him about. He said he belonged to a very conservative church now (I think he had been a Lutheran); in fact, he said he guessed he was part of the "religious right" (that is currently working behind the scenes so much today.) He didn't seem offended when I sort of raised my eyebrows, but he was quick to say it was mainly his wife's doing. Most of the people were Republicans, too - the same people who, along with their parents, had been Democrats in the forties and fifties. There was still a lot of racial stereotyping when talking about Hurricane Katrina and New Orleans, just as I remember its being years ago.

I visited the home of one of my friends I had known since the second grade. In fact, I had met him when his mother had asked me to help him with his spelling, since he was having so much trouble with it. It was a beautiful home with all new furnishings, and his back lawn sloped down to a lake, which he told me contained an alligator, but a friendly one. Long divorced, he had recently remarried. Another friend, who had been a neighbor when I was in grammar school, came by my sister's home with her husband, who was a prominent architect. They both looked great and seemed quite happy.

The Colts were playing the Jaguars in Jacksonville on Sunday and although I'm not a big sports fan, I really liked the fact that the Colts won and that the local newspaper had a front page article the next day criticizing the Jaguars' coach and a player for being bad sports.

Everyone's life has had its ups and downs and most were willing to be more frank and honest than I would have thought at a reunion, although many of these people had kept in touch with each other and had run into each other in their work or social lives all through the years. No one longed for or seemed nostalgic about the high school days but most seemed genuinely interested in the others, so much so that our luncheon ran on until past 4:00 PM.

I had a great visit and arrived non-stop back in Indianapolis just in time for another blast of wintry weather.

Inner Sanctum

Evolution has determined that for the continued survival of the human species, one of man's sexual glands, the prostate, be hidden away in the most inaccessible part of his body. It can only be approached by going up a path that things should only go down. Modern medical doctors, not to be outdone by millions of years of the evolutionary process, have figured out a way to get to it, however, not always for the survival of the species, either, since it is mainly elderly men who seem to get prostate problems.

After the age of fifty, most men have an enlarged prostate gland, just as they become bald, get grey hair or wrinkles, or get a pot belly. Most men have no particular symptoms except as the years progress, like many women, too, they have to make more frequent trips to the bathroom. In later years, many men, if not most, get cancer of the prostate, although it is a slow-growing kind, and they usually end up dying of something else long before the cancer gets them or spreads to other parts of the body.

If you're wondering why you're getting a lecture on urology it's because I recently had my annual physical examination, although it had been closer to a year and a half since the previous one. My general practitioner had me go through a number of tasks and tests that he thought would tell him something about my physical condition. He had me push against his hands as hard as I could and touch my finger to my nose with my eyes closed and watched me walk across the examining room. He knew better than to try to assess my mental condition, so he didn't have me count backward from 100 by 7's or ask who the president is, and it's a good thing, too, because my blood pressure would surely have shot up just mentioning Bush's name. After listening to me breathe and pounding all around on my chest and back with a little rubber hammer, he informed me that it was now time for the part that he knows I've been waiting anxiously for - the manual examination of my prostate.

He then informed me that I seemed to be in a healthy condition, noting the twenty pounds that I'd recently lost, saying he assumes I lost it on purpose. Well, duh! He then said that was fine and that the blood tests, for which I'd earlier given three test tubes of blood, would probably be back in several days, but that I should probably wait a week to call in for the results, just to make sure he'd had time to look at them.

Since I always go to his office to get a copy of my test results, I got a little anxious when the nurse told me he said to put me in a room and he'd give me the results. He went over all the results as if looking at them for the first time, saying that nothing appeared out of order except my PSA test, the one for indicating possible problems with the prostate, was slightly elevated. He said just to be on the safe side (I think he meant for himself, not me) he was going to refer me to a urologist. I told him the name of the one I'd been to many years ago, and he said he went to a urologist in the same practice. I called and tried to make an appointment with the guy I'd had before and was told it would be over a month, so I asked about the one my own doctor had seen, and I was told that he had just had a cancellation for the next Friday and could see me then.

Of course the first thing a urologist does is to conduct his own examination. He didn't find anything alarming, but said just to be on the safe side (again, I think he meant his) that I should have a biopsy done. I asked about pain, but he told me I wouldn't feel a thing, as they would give me a prostate block. I arranged for the biopsy and was told I could drive myself there and back as the procedure would only take about five minutes and be done in the office.

As I was lying only half naked on the examining table and carefully draped, the doctor came in and said that a local anesthetic would be administered first and there would be a little sting. He then said not to be alarmed by a rather loud popping noise when he did each of the biopsies. I repeated his last phrase, "… each of the biopsies?" "Yes," he said. He would do four on one side and four on the other side of the prostate. That was the first time I had heard that, and if I hadn't already been half naked on the table, I would have left right then. However, although the procedure was certainly uncomfortable, I really didn't feel any pain. Afterwards, I got dressed and went out to make a return appointment and was told that because of the Labor Day holiday, I would probably have to wait two weeks to get the results. I asked if I could call in on the next Friday, just in case and was told, rather perfunctorily I thought, that I could try but there were no promises the results would be back by then.

Of course after a week of anxious waiting and reading everything I could on the Internet (sometimes comforting and sometimes anxiety-arousing) I called the next week and left a message with the doctor's assistant to call me with the results if they did get them back and had a chance to go over them. In the late afternoon, I did get a call, telling me that my results were back and that all eight biopsies were negative. I had her repeat that, as I wanted to make sure I had heard correctly. It was like having a life sentence lifted or at least changed to probation. I then asked what my "Gleason score" was, an indicator of how fast the cancer is growing or how serious the condition is that I had learned from several reliable sources on the Internet. She told me I didn't have a Gleason score - since everything had been negative. I really felt relief then for the first time in weeks. She told me to make a follow-up appointment in a couple of months to be seen again in six months. I don't think so - my annual physical examination with my good old GP is going to be enough for me from now on. Just call me a wuss.

Dos and Don'ts

Eats lots of broccoli, drink ten or twelve glasses of water a day, exercise, get plenty of rest, don't drive too fast, don't eat too many sweets, have a close group of friends with whom you talk and socialize, stay informed on political matters, give of yourself, get your finances in order, if you already have a will, make sure it's updated, don't go into debt, stay active and enthusiastic, work Sudoku puzzles so that your brain doesn't atrophy - well, you get the point.

It seems everyone wants to tell us what to do today - what's healthy for us, what isn't. We had a friend once who was so conscientious about exercise and what she ate that it didn't seem as though she was having much fun. She said she was going to follow all these instructions, but when she was 65 and retired, she was going to start eating all the things she wasn't supposed to and start enjoying life, because by then she thought she would have earned it and it probably wouldn't hurt then, either. Well, she did all those things, but they never really became an entrenched part of her life, and just before she retired, she had a serious heart attack. She recovered, though, probably due to her eating all those steamed vegetables that had no taste, and lived long enough to have had back surgery twice, another heart attack, a stroke from which she may never recover fully and now diabetes and an even more stringent diet and lifestyle.

Sometimes I get the feeling that it just isn't worth all the trouble to watch out for all the things that could get you. But, of course, I happen to like vegetables, and salads, and fish, and even exercise. I think, in fact, that I haven't led a life as adventuresome as I should have. A friend whom I haven't seen since 1959 and I started e-mailing each other and talking on the phone occasionally. She'd been planning a trip to Bucharest to visit some friends whom she had made when she worked in Germany several years in the 1960's. A few months ago she planned a trip by boat up the Danube and was almost set to go when she saw on TV the other day that the Danube was flooding very badly. Well, it turns out the trip had to be cancelled, so she decided to visit the same friend who has a daughter and son-in-law in Switzerland. She asked why didn't I join her and spend a couple of weeks in Zurich? She didn't mean anything romantic about our traveling together - just as a couple of old friends.

Well, I don't even have a passport now, but as exciting as it sounds, I told her I didn't think so. See what I mean by not being adventuresome? It's about all I can do to plan a trip to Florida in June and a trip to Tennessee in October. I've even put off getting another cat until after I return from my October trip to the National Storytelling Festival, as I didn't want to have to board a new pet while I was gone.

I know I whine too much and that I really am fortunate in a lot of ways. One gets used to a routine and then it seems more comfortable not to veer from it, even though it might be boring at times. I probably do too much planning and not enough doing. It's difficult to be spontaneous when you get older, or at least I find it so. I did sign up for a course offered by IUPUI at Glendale for the next five Mondays, which means I won't be able to stick with my routine of going to the Avon Scrabble Club for the next five weeks, and maybe that's a good thing. After all, I can see many of the same players on Thursday nights at the club that meets on the northwest side of town.

I got something in the mail today that seemed adventuresome I'm sure for the women who participated in it - a bunch of elderly women posed nude for a calendar to raise money to try to save an old courthouse from being torn down. The calendar was bought and sent to me by a Scrabble player in Muncie, who has been widowed recently.

I didn't know exactly how to finish this little masterpiece, so I left it on my computer while I read about twenty pages to finish a book I had from the library. What the main character says in the last few pages gave me an idea for a project that will take at least a couple of months to complete, but you'll be hearing more about it, so I won't tell you what it is. I think it might just get me out of the doldrums.

The Autumn of My Life

Autumn used to be my favorite season, and maybe it still is. I like to see the trees turn various shades of red, yellow, and gold. I really like Indian summer, when there are days of high temperatures and blue skies with white puffy clouds - days I thought were over until next year. It's like a bonus - something given to me that I hadn't quite expected. When I lived in Florida, spring used to be my favorite time of the year, but that was because I'd never seen a real autumn. Many of the oak trees in Florida never lose all their leaves, and palms don't either, of course.

I guess I'm in the autumn of my life now, so it seems I should be more satisfied with my life than I am. I wrote a previous memoir that included a quote from George Sheehan's book that said he thought the goal of life was to be happy - not good, but happy, because one could be good by just doing nothing - not stealing, not killing, etc., whereas one first had to do something to engage in some action, to be happy. It was only the result of some action that one knew happiness. This made sense at the time I read it, and perhaps it is true, but one can engage in a lot of actions and do things and go places and still not be happy. So, of course, it must depend on the motivation of the person and some other factors, too. Maybe the things one does have to be "good" things or helpful activities - for good causes or charities or disaster relief. What happens if one does the right things but for the wrong reasons?

I thought life would get less complicated and simpler as one gets older, but I haven't found that to be true. I always thought that the main reason people are unhappy is that they have unrealistic expectations and that if one could just modify their expectations to be more realistic, then one wouldn't be unhappy. I still think this is true to a great extent.

I've been seeing a lot of movies recently because that is something I enjoy. I just saw *Capote,* and Truman Capote was shown to be a manipulative, selfish person who would do almost anything to get what he wanted. At first, he obtained a lawyer for the two men convicted of killing a Kansas family so that they would be around long enough for him to gather all the facts that he thought he needed to write *In Cold Blood,* which later made him the most famous writer alive at the time. Then there were so many appeals and the years kept rolling by, and he couldn't finish the book because he didn't know how it would end, that he stopped trying to help the murderers, even though he felt a great kinship with one of them. He said it was like they (meaning him and one of the murderers) had both grown up in the same orphanage, but that he left by the front door and the murderer left by the back door. After becoming even more famous after the book was published, he never finished writing another book. The other recent movies I've seen have had similarly depressing themes, so one of my favorite pastimes isn't being very helpful. I've always thought that one can't actually look for happiness. It's like a by-product that happens when doing something else.

So, foolhardily, perhaps, when I was asked to take the place of a member on the Homeowners' Association Board who is moving, I agreed. Now my previous times on the board weren't the most happy, and although it's a job most people don't want, I think it is very necessary and will help protect my investment, if nothing else. One reason they asked me is that they want me to do the bimonthly Newsletter. Now, I definitely won't be able to put off buying a new computer any longer, something I've procrastinated about for months.

I've also planned a trip to Florida in early December to visit my sister and brother-in-law, who have just moved into a new home. I'll get to attend the 53rd high school Christmas reunion luncheon. There will be around fifty people there from my graduating class. I haven't seen anyone from my class since I went to the 35th reunion.

Who knows, maybe I'll find I like Florida so much that I'll think about moving back. I don't really consider that anything more than a possibility, though, since there are too many people I like here and too many things I still don't like about the South, and I'm not talking just about hurricanes, either. So, you may have to put up with me for another few autumns until winter comes - several years down the road.

Whiskey, Tango, Foxtrot

I was driving home from the last memoirs group and listening to NPR. A photojournalist was being interviewed about his new book that contained images of the war in Iraq from 2002 through 2006. He'd become very disillusioned by the war. At first, he was all for the war and tried to put a human face and give a human voice to the Iraqi civilians and to the American soldiers fighting and occupying Iraq. But as the insurgencies and casualties wore on and the occupation continued, he felt he was more of an archivist, just chronicling the demise of a nation and how futile it all seemed. Although he was now only twenty-seven, he sounded like a much older, world-weary man.

He told a story of our troops isolating a farm house thought to be used to harbor terrorists, filling it with explosives and getting ready to blow it up. As this was proceeding, a Humvee came along the road headed right past the house, but the communications were down, and they couldn't radio it that the house was about to explode. Finally, one soldier ran out and signaled it, and it turned around just as bricks and beams started flying through the air a few feet away. Then, the staticky radio came to life, and the operator of the Humvee yelled, Whiskey, Tango, Foxtrot ?—a code phrase meaning, "What the...f---?"—used when no one knew what the hell was going on.

I sometimes feel like yelling Whiskey, Tango, Foxtrot. Part of the trouble I'm having now is because I'm president of the homeowners' association board where I live. What I thought would be a few hours of volunteer work a month is turning into a 20-hour a week, part-time job - with no benefits.

The reason I moved to a condo in the first place was to avoid the hassles of having responsibility for all the outside maintenance on a big house and yard. Now, though, I have to be concerned about the roofing, painting, landscaping, snow removal, pool upkeep, clubhouse repairs, etc. of 174 units. This is all done with the help of other board members, a property manager, and a bunch of contractors. Since there's only one board meeting a month, I regularly receive irate e-mails or telephone calls from angry residents or those who like to whine and complain about the smallest things, without any idea of the big picture.

When I got back from a recent trip to Florida, not only were there e-mails and messages on the answering machine but notes left under my front door mat. Some - many, actually - are legitimate complaints, but they should be addressed to the property manager at the management company, not to someone on the board. On the other hand, we do get volunteers who help distribute the quarterly newsletter or who want to help by planting flowers in the three big pots around the pool, and they do a good job.

Earlier this summer, we had a woman who screamed she was being attacked by a dog, when actually, the dog was more romantically interested in the dog she was walking, - there were witnesses who saw the whole thing. The owner who tethered his dog outside was fined, because the dog could easily get loose if excited.

Most mornings I read the *Star* over breakfast, and my reaction is Whiskey, Tango, Foxtrot. I heard, again on NPR, that we're paying an off-shoot of Halliburton a half-billion dollars a month to supply logistics to our military personnel. Some of my fellow Scrabble Club members who live in Washington township had their taxes increased up to 100 %, and that certainly merits a W., T., F?

I saw *Sicko*, the new movie by Michael Moore, the other night, and my reaction again was, W, T, F?

I'm going to google W, T, F? on the internet and see if there's a cure for it. Of course, it probably won't be covered by Medicare or my AARP supplement.

Coming Attractions

I've always enjoyed watching the previews when we go to movie theaters. It's as though you're getting something extra - a sample of something you didn't have to pay for. I used to spend a dime on Saturdays to see a double feature - usually a new movie that had already been at a downtown first-run theater, and a B-movie, usually a Western or a murder mystery. Of course, we also had at least one cartoon, a March of Time newsreel, sometimes a short documentary, and then several previews--of coming attractions.

I think it was Ted Turner who said, "Life is like a B-movie; I wouldn't want to miss any of it, but I sure wouldn't want to sit through it again, either." I'm not quite that cynical. But it seems to me that life is really a lot like going to the movies on a Saturday afternoon used to be - a little news - information/education you might need; a cartoon or two - to show you the funny side of life; a B-movie - some fantasy thrown in to contrast with the *big picture* - the feature-length film with lots of drama, odd characters, theme music, nature, a story. But what about coming attractions of your life? How would it be to get titillating glimpses of what your life might be in the next few months or even years? Different versions, maybe even an R or X-rated version as well as a PG - hardly ever is life a G rating anymore. Would they help anyone? Even if you knew what was going to happen, would you be able to change it - say, give it a happy ending, rather than the one shown? Sequels would be almost mandatory - including issues you didn't settle earlier in life.

Who would be the stars of your life - your movie? I guess you'd be the main character - or would you be the director? Who would the screenwriter be? Could you bring in a script doctor? Would the audience approve? Maybe this is taking the analogy too far - would it win an Academy Award? Would it make money? Would you want to get up and walk out? Would you rather wait until it got to DVD to see it? What would the critics say? Unbelievable? Whom would you thank for an award? Your parents or a teacher?

This is just a preview, a coming attraction - so don't expect closure.

Printed in the United States
139700LV00002B/4/P

9 781440 121548